John 3:16
by C. Matthew McMahon

Copyright Information

John 3:16 by C. Matthew McMahon
Edited by Therese B. McMahon

Revised, Second Edition Copyright ©2021 by Puritan Publications and A Puritan's Mind®

Some language and grammar are updated from any original manuscripts. Any change in wording or punctuation has not changed the intent or meaning of the original author(s) and has been made to aid the modern reader.

Published by Puritan Publications
A Ministry of A Puritan's Mind® in Crossville, TN.
www.apuritansmind.com
www.puritanpublications.com

All rights reserved. No part of this publication may be reproduced, stored in a retrieval system or transmitted in any form by any means, electronic, mechanical, photocopy, recording or otherwise, without the prior permission of the publisher, except as provided by USA copyright law.

This Second Print Edition, 2021
Second Electronic Edition, 2021
Manufactured in the United States of America

ISBN: 978-1-62663-178-6
eISBN: 978-1-62663-177-9

Table of Contents

Introduction 4
Part 1: John 2:23-3:1 13
    Study Questions for Part 1 19
Part 2: John 3:1 20
    Study Questions for Part 2 23
Part 3: John 3:2-10 24
    Study Questions for Part 3 43
Part 4: John 3:11-15 44
    Study Questions for Part 4 54
Part 5: John 3:16 55
    Study Questions for Part 5 92
Part 6: John 3:17-21 94
    Study Questions for Part 6 101
Part 7: Final Thoughts 102
Part 8: Your Spiritual Birth 106
Other Helpful Books Published by Puritan Publications 122

Introduction

There is no other passage of Scripture quoted more extensively throughout church history than John 3:16. By default, there is no other Scripture quoted or explained more *incorrectly* than John 3:16, *especially* in our own day. By consequence, the most *abused verse* in the entire bible is John 3:16. Though hearty appeal is made to the love of God for the world (many times stated and preached by ministers with the greatest of intentions), far less do people hermeneutically and theologically understand the ideas and textural concerns about the passage as a whole in its immediate context, and especially its greater biblical context. Subsequently, ignorance is blinding in today's interpretive view of the difficult theological concept of *God's love to the world.* Those people who often quote this verse think they understand this passage because they *believe* it is so plain. In other words, the way it is written (in English), is the way it should be understood – it seems plain enough, doesn't it? Scripture, to most professing Christian laymen and pastors, *seems* straight forward. And what could be more straightforward as the desire to have *God love us*, and say just *that* in this verse as plainly and absolutely as Jesus seems to say it to Nicodemus?

In hermeneutics, one of the more abused rules is the affinity that people have to the plain meaning of the text. In other words, hermeneutics *certainly* teaches us that we ought to hold to the plain meaning of the text. What is overlooked, is that *to get to* the plain meaning of the text, does not mean to simply read it, but to know what its meaning actually teaches. The plain reading of the text is not always so clear, and can hold lots of assumptions if we deal with it irresponsibly.[1] John 3:16 seems to be straightforward in this, that hermeneutical rules are often tossed aside, because one cursory reading of the verse causes professing Christians to be persuaded by the "divine truth" that God loves them, because he loves the world. And when they take such a shortcut to understanding a passage (any Scriptural passage) they retain an assumed man-centeredness to it rather than a God or Christ-centeredness to its interpretation. With most professing believers today in the current Evangelical church, John 3:16 boils down to a verse that essentially offers *a way to be saved* because

---

[1] In Isaiah, God says, "those who rejoice in my triumph." Shall we read this with preconceived notions, and let the text simply say what it says? Let's be silly, even irresponsible, for a moment, with our hermeneutics, and ask, *Does this mean that God owns a Triumph Triple 1200 S motorcycle and that there are people who rejoice that God owns such a vehicle, or must we be more careful in our understanding of the word triumph?* Truly, God does *not* ride on motorcycles called "Triumphs." That would be an abuse of letting the text speak for itself, especially for all motorcycle enthusiasts who read the bible.

Introduction

God loves me so much, because, *he loves the whole world.*

The professing Christian may be thinking, "God loves me because he says he loves me in John 3:16." I'd ask, "How do you come to that conclusion?" They think, "God loves me because I am part of the "world" in which he loves. And, so, because he loves the world, he loves me too. God loves everyone, right?" To enhance this line of thought, it is not simply in an abstract idea that *God loves*, but *he loved the world so much* that he sent his one and only Son to die on behalf of the world, or so it seems. So, the professing believer thinks, "God loves me so much that he sent his Son to die for me." Why? They answer, "I am part of the world, and God loves the world, and he loves the world so much that Christ died for the world, and so, he died for me because I am part of that world, and that makes me feel good to think that I am part of the world that God loves." To press this even further, most professing Christians who read John 3:16 do so at the expense of the passage in which it sits, and they make no relationship from this verse, to any other verse in the passage or discourse between Jesus and Nicodemus. John 3:16 is *so* clear, (they believe), that there is no need to do anything more than simply read the words aloud for them to hear in their ears; so they subconsciously, or even consciously, think in this way that by merely reading the verse, it must mean what it says (again, in English as they read it).[2] It is almost as if they suppose, "*Everyone* thinks this way about the passage because it is so simple and straightforward. I am thinking about it that way as well." They believe John 3:16 is so plain that there is little to nothing the reader necessarily needs to do in order to understand that, 1) God loves, 2) that God loves the world, 3) that they are part of that whole which God loves, 4) that God loves the world and those who are part of the world so much that he sent his Son on their behalf, and, 5) that the Son of God died on behalf of the world that God loves. But in considering this passage, there is *more.* God says in this same verse that "whosoever believes" this is saved, and will not perish, and *will have* everlasting life. So they may think, "God so loves the world, and I am in the world, so God loves me, and he sent his Son to die for the world, and that means me as well; what shall I conclude form all this? I will conclude that whosoever believes this will be saved. And, I believe this, so I am saved and will have everlasting life." This is the most common interpretation of this verse in our own day. But our day is captive to a whole host of erroneous ideas concerning God, Christ, salvation and yes, John 3:16. Should erroneous modern opinions be considered in light of any verse we interpret? The church today as a whole has been so conditioned by what we will call "easy

---

[2] Does John 3:16 read the same way in Turkish? Albanian? Japanese?

believism," that they have a difficult time seeing the text of John 3:16 as anything but what is commonly read and popularly believed as the simple Gospel. What does the football patron mean when he holds up a sign that has written on it, "JOHN 3:16," during the game on Sunday, when he's engaging in Sabbath-breaking at the expense to hold up a sign at the big game? The theology of the contemporary church sits squarely in doing whatever is expedient; whatever works according to their own agenda. And the Evangelical church today is content to believe in the simplicity of John 3:16, so much so, that all they need to do is hold up a sign to Sabbath-breaking football players and patrons who can read the verse, and they too can know that God loves them, and gave Christ for them. The question is then asked, why would I want to make all this more difficult in writing a whole book on one verse to understand John 3:16 when it is so plain that even carnal football players know what it means when signs are held up that God loves them, and everyone else?

If you ask me what my favorite bible verse is, it is John 3:16. My favorite passage is John 3:1-21, because this was the verse God used to convert me. We tend to have an affinity to verses and preachers that God uses in our conversion. I don't single out this verse and passage at the expense of the rest of the bible, or simply because I wrote this study book on the verse. Rather, I think the rest of the bible fuels this section of Scripture, and I believe Christ's summation of God's manner of salvation can be found here in all its fullness, among other important doctrinal points in this verse.[3] Having said that, it is difficult to see the warped and misused interpretation of this passage which occurs in the hands of most professing Christians today.

John 3:16, for me, is one of those life-verses I learned at an early age, and it came to blossom for me in my early days in Bible college. In my first summer there, I needed to choose a topic to personally study while in between classes for the Summer. In doing so I defaulted to John 3:16. I was greatly compelled (at this particular point in my Christian walk) to radically understand the death of Christ *for me*. What did that really mean? What were the implications of that for me? So, I embarked on a study that would fundamentally change the way I viewed the love of God, the death of his Son, and the manner in which I was saved and converted. The study so profoundly changed my view of these theological concepts, that I tailored the next few years of my education to deal with concepts that directly related to this study in order to expound it more readily. Regardless of the class or course of study I was in at the time, I was writing assignments and papers that

---

[3] See my work, *The Five Principles of the Gospel* in expanding that idea.

specifically had to do with this biblical text, and with theological concepts that stem from the text. After Bible college I tailored my seminary studies to fit the theological slant of various ideas I gleaned from John 3:16, many of which were ideas housed in systematic theology. Consequently, I drafted my thesis for my master's degree around *the atonement*. This was further work which pressed me to consider *why Christ died for me, personally*. Later on, that master's thesis would in turn become a full-orbed Ph.D. work called, "The Two Wills of God." It takes the theological implications of the atonement of Christ, and stretches it out into various theological areas that concern God's work in redemption and salvation, and how that concept should be preached, and how it should be understood by believers.[4] In doing this, my objective was to gather and incorporate as much theological study as I could to explain the biblical view of Christ's words in John 3:16, and successively treat *historical theology* alongside of it (a topic that is supremely neglected in the church today). What did the Christian church, throughout church history, believe concerning John 3:16 and its meaning? Is today's understanding of John 3:16 and its context the same as what the church had always taught? Or, has the church today changed this verse in some

---

[4] That Ph.D. dissertation has also been shortened and updated into the book *The Two Wills of God Made Easy*.

way? So we come to this work which, for today's Christian reader, I've boiled down decades of reading into relatively few pages, explaining and citing what I think is most pertinent to understanding my favorite verse in the Bible.

Not only will this book deal with the text, but at the end of each chapter I'm going to incorporate some study questions for personal interaction by you, the reader. That way the content of the book is not simply threaded through your eyes as you read, but that it might work its way into your heart as well by pondering those questions. What Christian doesn't want to understand John 3:16 more fully? Or for that matter, who would not want to understand what Jesus truly *meant* when our Savior explained *salvation* in this context? And by the time we finish this interactive study, my desire is that you might have come to greater, more precise and accurate understanding of Christ's words in one of the most, if not the most, beloved passage in all the bible.

I also want to draw your attention to the relatively "light" parts of this book that come before and after Part 5 which concerns John 3:16. In part 5, I will not only demonstrate the meaning of the passage exegetically, but also historically. There are quite a few quotes, and many footnotes that will enhance the study further than the light reading of the other parts of this work. But once you, the reader, get involved in that chapter, don't become overwhelmed. Simply follow along and slowly deal with the quotes, language study and exegetical work that are offered there. That way you will not only have a good idea about what Christ means in John 3:16, but also the theological history that surrounds its interpretation by sound pastors, theologians and divines.

Lastly, the second edition of this book has been enlarged by ten pages, and has added a number of resources throughout (a large amount of added footnotes), as well as some important accompaniments to understanding John 3:16 as it pertains to other recommended books and writers.

Part 1:
John 2:23-3:1

"Now when he was in Jerusalem at the Passover, in the feast day, many believed in his name, when they saw the miracles which he did. But Jesus did not commit himself unto them, because he knew all men, and needed not that any should testify of man: for he knew what was in man," (John 2:23-25).

As much as we would like to open our Bibles to John 3:16 and start *there*, we cannot. In understanding John 3:16, we actually need to start in John 2:23 through to John 3:1.[1] In John 2 there are two important narratives

---

[1] Keep in mind that the Bible does *not* start with John 3:16. The Bible starts with Genesis 1:1 and first assumes the reader is acquainted with the God who created heaven and earth, his kingdom, his Gospel, and then, it takes quite a long time, and many theological ideas and prescriptions given to the church, for God to ultimately send his one and only Son into the physical world at a particular time in history as the Messiah who fulfills the Gospel (see my works, *The Kingdom of Heaven is Upon You* and *The Lord's Voice Cries in the City* for a full study on the topic of God's Gospel message. The careful Bible student will begin with reading the Scriptures of the Old Testament (remembering that every time *Christ* references the Scriptures, he was speaking about the Old Testament which was his Bible, which we will consider when we look at John 3:10). In order to understand the Gospel of John as a whole, much less the rest of the New Testament, one must start with where God started, which was in the Old Testament. The New Testament is not understandable without the Old Testament, and the Old Testament is not fulfilled, and covenantally complete, without the New Testament. For our purposes, we must keep this

mentioned. The first is the wedding at Cana, and the second is the cleansing of the temple. Much could be said about both of these sections. It is not my intention to give you a full-length exegetical commentary on these passages, or for that matter, on all of John 3. I do, though, want to bring to your intention important points that drive the force of Christ's instruction to Nicodemus once we begin reading John 3.

For our study, it is important to note that John mentions the wedding miracles in this way, "This beginning of miracles did Jesus in Cana of Galilee, and manifested forth his glory; and his disciples believed on him," (John 2:11). Miracles and signs are important theological ideas in laying out the coming passage. Christ accomplished the miracle of changing water to wine, and then he pressed for outward reformation in cleansing the temple. You might wonder why cleansing the temple is a sign or miracle. It is not, but the temple cleansing set the stage for a short teaching on his own resurrection; which is one of if not the greatest miracles recorded in the Gospels (they are linked). "Jesus answered and said unto them, Destroy this temple, and in three days I will raise it up." The text then reads, "Then said the Jews, Forty and six years was this temple in building, and wilt thou rear it up in three days? But he

---

study in its respective context, which means we must look at very important words like, "Now," as we begin in John chapter 2.

spake of the temple of his body. When therefore he was risen from the dead, his disciples remembered that he had said this unto them; and they believed the scripture, and the word which Jesus had said," (John 2:19-22). These two important narratives set the stage for John's continued narrative in 2:23-3:21.

After these two historical accounts, we come to the important transition of the transition of, "now," in John 2:23. "*Now* when he was in Jerusalem at the Passover, in the feast day, many believed in his name, when they saw the miracles which he did. But Jesus did not commit himself unto them, because he knew all men, and needed not that any should testify of man: for he knew what was in man," (John 2:23-25). The transition is a type of commentary. John tells us that as a result of these miracles and teachings, many believed in his name. He says *they believed* in his name, "when they *saw* the miracles which he did." However, it is important to remember that miracles *do not give people saving faith.* They may be a means the Holy Spirit uses to engage people in the truth of the Messiah during the time of Christ and the Apostles, but they are not the regenerating power used to *change* people. Transformation is the work of the Holy Spirit in the use of the word of God applied in regeneration to a person's heart. As a matter of fact, this commentary, then, sets the stage very nicely for the explanation of what it means to be saved in the discourse Christ has with Nicodemus. Actually, we see in the first interaction with Christ, Nicodemus uses the notation on the "signs" that Jesus accomplished in public view as a confirmation that he comes from God.[2] But Jesus, as we will see, quickly changes the conversation to deal directly with the manner in which people truly see and become converted. Let's hold that thought for the time being.

The word "now" that transitions into Christ's Nicodemus discourse is a Greek word John uses quite often meaning, "moreover." We might say today, "as a result of all this," such and such should be noted. This is John's intention in the transition. People followed Christ outwardly because they saw what he did. But John's further commentary enlightens the reality that these people were not converted. Belief, in this case, was outward, or nominal. As a result of this, "Jesus did not commit himself unto them, because he knew all men, and needed not that any should testify of man: for he knew what was in man," (John 2:24-25). Christ would not commit himself to them, even though they

---

[2] "For no man can do these miracles that thou dost, except God be with him." "As if he had said, whoever works miracles, comes from God, but you work miracles, therefore you come from God. This clause, "these miracles thou dost," carries a great emphasis, and shows that they were very great miracles which Christ did, and confirms the argument all the more. This reason is sound, and affords this point of doctrine, that miracles cannot be wrought but by divine power." Gouge, Thomas, *The Works of Thomas Gouge*, (E & E Hosford, 1815) 14.

committed themselves, in a certain respect, to him. Why? Christ saw clearly what was in the heart of men. He knew the depth of their depravity, and understood clearly that in order for people to truly commit to him, the Holy Spirit must first do a special work in them so that their belief would extend into true faith. This is something they could not do on their own. This is something that had *not* happened to them yet. John tells us that they *believed* because they *saw* what he did. All their pandering was outward. But Christ is more concerned with the inward disposition of the fallen heart, and how that heart must be changed in order to rightly and successfully believe in him. *That means saving faith and belief is not predicated on Christ's outward supernatural works merely seen. Something more must first take place in order for those believing to believe rightly, to the saving of their souls.* This is going to be strikingly prevalent when Jesus speaks with Nicodemus in the next few verses.

You might ask, "How is nominal belief on Christ wrong?" Any belief that can be rivaled by the demons who ultimately will wind up in hell is not useful. The demons believe in Christ and tremble, but they are not converted (*cf.* "the devils also believe, and tremble," (James 2:19)). People must have a different kind of "believing" than the demons have. Thomas Hodges, Westminster divine said, "Devils tremble, men quake," (*cf.* James 2:19, Isaiah 33:14); and they are like the worms who wriggle into the corners of the earth when it thunders. So all men are like this."[3] Such unconverted people are worse than the demons who, "believe God's threats and tremble at his wrath."[4]

---

[3] Hodges, Thomas, *A Glimpse of God's Glory*, (Crossville, TN: Puritan Publications, 2017) see his section on God's Loftiness.
[4] Price, William, *The Soul's Porter, or a Treatise on the Fear of God*, (Coconut Creek, FL: Puritan Publications, 2012), see chapter 11, *A dissuasion from those sins that are contrary to the fear of God. And first of carnal security, with the remedy of it.*

Study Questions for Part 1

1. Why did Jesus *not commit* himself to those who believed in him because of his miracles?

2. What kind of belief do demons have?

3. People believed in Christ because he did miracles, and they were following him as a result of what they saw. Why is believing *something* about Christ, even if it is the truth, not enough for Jesus to commit himself to them? Why does *Christ think* this is not enough for him to commit himself to the people?

4. Why does sin (the baseness of the heart of a man) play an important part in their salvation according to John 2:23-3:1?

5. What miracles or signs did the people outwardly see and trust in to follow Christ the way they did?

Part 2:
John 3:1

"There was a man of the Pharisees, named Nicodemus, a ruler of the Jews," (John 3:1).

When we begin John chapter 3, we find this is a continuation of the transition by John in 2:23. This discussion and discourse is a direct result of seeing Christ's miracles and work previously mentioned before the "now" of the transition to this passage. The passage in John 3, for our purposes, should be divided up into three sections. The first section is verse 1, which introduces Nicodemus in the narrative. The second section is verses 2-10 which is a dialogue between Jesus and Nicodemus. Then we have verses 11-21 which is now a discourse *to* Nicodemus.

Another note to keep in mind is the transition from the previous chapter to this one concerning seeing and believing in John 2, which was particular to the *crowd*, and is now applied to an *individual*. Jesus takes the time, that he did not take with the crowd, to speak with Nicodemus.

We should note at the outset that Nicodemus is a Pharisee. The Pharisees were rulers or teachers of the people of Israel who were birthed out of a time just previous to the Maccabean wars. They were sticklers for doctrine, interestingly enough, and they had many theological truths correct, such as their teaching on the resurrection of the body. However, their fatal flaw was that they externalized religion. They conformed to ideas and precepts which outwardly gave the appearance of piety and religion. Do you see a theme running through here? In John 2:23ff people saw, *outwardly*, the works of Christ, and they committed themselves to him because they saw these outward works. Nicodemus is an outward keeper of the law (or his perception of what law-keeping meant to the Jews at the time). The Pharisees concocted special extra-biblical laws to keep themselves safe from the "sinful" culture in which they lived. Nicodemus will even flatter Christ with "seeing" the great works Jesus does and concludes he must be of God because he does all these outward works which seem to speak to keeping the law of God in a holy manner. All this *outward* religiosity is what prompts not only the Spirit's divine inspired word in the narrative we have in John 3, but specifically of Christ's response to Nicodemus.

Nicodemus, being a Pharisee, would also have been a member of the Sanhedrin as well as a scribe. He was a "ruler of the Jews" which is a direct title to the Sanhedrin, those who ruled the Jews from the appearance of religion. They were teachers of the Law (at that time such comprised the Hebrew Scriptures which was Christ's Bible) comprising the 39 books or writings of the Old Testament in the Law, Writings and the Prophets. He would have also been an interpreter of the Scriptures, a student of Hebrew and scholar who should have been exceedingly familiar with the important theological doctrines that the people of Israel should have been taught first hand concerning the manner in which people were to live before God; *i.e.* following God's holy Law. This will be a striking rebuke once we consider verse 10. Jesus will call into question Nicodemus' credentials and position based on his ignorance to the authoritative word that he actually knows little to nothing about.

Study Questions for Part 2

1. What are the three sections that divide up John 3:1-21, and why is this division important?

2. What was problem of the Pharisees in their attempt at obeying God?

3. What outward shows of religion do you see today in the contemporary church that attract unconverted people to attend church services?

4. What is the importance of seeing and believing for the crowd, and for the Pharisee, Nicodemus?

Part 3:
John 3:2-10

"The same came to Jesus by night, and said unto him, Rabbi, we know that thou art a teacher come from God: for no man can do these miracles that thou doest, except God be with him," (John 3:2).

We know nothing about Nicodemus other than what is given to us here in the Gospel of John. There is a mentioning of a Nicodemus in secular Greek literature about this time, but it has little to do with what we know about this biblical narrative and any type of history behind this specific figure. We simply have what is written here, and in two other sections in the Gospel of John, which we will treat later on.

Nicodemus, a ruler (or teacher) of the Jews, approaches Jesus "by night..." It would not be profitable for the Pharisee to be seen with Jesus during the day since the other Pharisees were hostile to Christ. In some measure, there had to be shame in Nicodemus coming at such a time; shame for being seen with the disturber of the peace that the Pharisees so loved to harass and condemned. But there was something drawing Nicodemus to come to Christ, and speak with him. We can infer this based on the discourse and time Jesus takes in the next section (verses 11-21), and the time

Christ took to teach *regeneration* to Nicodemus. Visiting Christ by day would have brought Nicodemus a reproach among his sect. He was risking his own reputation by being seen with Christ, so, he comes under the cover of night. Isn't that typical of the way people often operate under the fear of men? Nicodemus was a professional in terms of outward religiosity. But when it comes to *true* religion, he is ashamed to be seen talking with the Savior. No doubt, he would have thought, "What will they say if they see me go to Jesus in public during the day? How will they reprimand *me?*" Nicodemus, at this point, takes the easier road. Still, his coming to Christ is something to be wondered at in and of itself. This Pharisee comes to the ridiculed rabbi to compliment him and attest that not only is his work from God, but that Christ, may in fact, be sent from God.

Secondly, Nicodemus compliments Jesus to gain his favor and show a "humble" sign of respect. Jesus must be a teacher come from God because, "no one can do these signs that You do unless God is with Him." Jesus heals the sick, causes lame people to walk again, cures the blind, deaf and dumb, and more. Look at all he can do! See what he has done. "Surely" if we *look and see* such things, our only conclusion must be that he is from God.[1]

---

[1] Keep in mind that even though Nicodemus is saying this to Jesus, he is not giving any type of consensus from the majority view of

Note three points here. Nicodemus, 1) calls Christ *rabbi*, 2) he believes that Christ is a teacher come *from God* based on what he has *seen* empirically, and, 3) he logically concludes that no man can do miracles, signs or wonders unless *God* was empowering him to do so. This is the beginning of what Nicodemus hoped to converse with Christ about.

1) Nicodemus calls Jesus Rabbi. The Greek term used is Ῥαββί, (rabbi) meaning *master* or *teacher*. However, it can be interpreted from Nicodemus' perspective as "my honorable sir,"[2] showing a more than civil sign of respect. Either way, Nicodemus is using this word as admiration. For not only is Christ honorable in Nicodemus' eyes, but he is also, 2) a teacher who has come from God. According to what this scribe, ruler and teacher of the Jews understands about the Hebrew Scriptures, such evidence of Christ's working miracles is a sure sign that he has been sent by God. Nicodemus misses the idea that outward religious signs or miracles do not necessarily mean that one is from God. Satan is a deceiver who attempts to demonstrate religious truth,

---

the Pharisees. They saw Christ as *opposed* to their religion because Christ was in fact opposed to their form of outward religiosity as supposed law-keepers.

[2] Suitable interpretations can mean, 1) my great one, my honorable sir 2) Rabbi, as a title used by the Jews to address their teachers (and also honor them when not addressing them).

in some ways, by signs and wonders.³ Nicodemus misses this idea completely, and, with the crowd, thinks that Christ is from God on the virtue of the ability *to be seen* doing such miracles. Nicodemus, 3) believes that the power to enact miracles is directly given by God. Christ is performing such miracles, not only in secret, or behind certain closed doors, but openly in the public view with thousands of people to attest to their veracity. They even engage in the application of the miracles in many instances; *i.e.* they drink the wine which was turned into wine from water, or they eat the fish and the loaves which were multiplied, *etc.*⁴

---

³ *cf.* "And the devil took him up and showed him all the kingdoms of the world in a moment of time," (Luke 4:5). "Satan disguises himself as an angel of light," (2 Cor. 11:14). "Put on the whole armor of God, that you may be able to stand against the schemes of the devil," (Eph. 6:11). "For they are demonic spirits, performing signs," (Rev. 16:14). "And the beast was captured, and with it the false prophet who in its presence had done the signs by which he received those who had received the mark of the beast and those who worshiped its image," (Rev. 19:20).

⁴ It is not my intention here to give a dissertation on miracles. That would sidetrack the study. But it would be a good point of research to see the differences between Christ's miracles and Satan's signs and wonders. Christ's miracles are used directly in conjunction with the Gospel message, by Christ or the Apostles, and ought to be defined as such. That in turn would remove the need to say things like, "It is a miracle Bob made it to the party," or, if a person is healed today in a hospital from cancer, that "They were healed and their healing is a miracle." Such "special providences" may certainly occur, but they are quite different than the evangelical message given by Christ or the Apostles to demonstrate the divinity and purpose of the Messiah's work and attestation of God's message.

Christ wastes no time with Nicodemus and does not readily acknowledge his compliments. Rather, Jesus says, "Most assuredly, I say to you, unless one is born again, he cannot see the Kingdom of God." This seems very out of place.[5] Why does Jesus immediately interrupt Nicodemus' compliments with talking about being born again? Is that really a logical answer? Yes, actually, it is. *Jesus is going to "fix" Nicodemus' understanding of what it means to equate seeing with believing.* The force behind "most assuredly" is as if Jesus was saying, "This is the way it is and you need to listen!" It is emphatic, used to grab the listener's (and reader's) attention, and acts as an exclamation mark to what is being stated. He then says, "Unless…" The word "unless" means, "something must absolutely happen before something else happens." Unless what? "Unless a man." The word "man" in this context refers to "a person." "Unless a person." The masculine words "man" or "men" are used to refer to mankind as a whole throughout

---

[5] "This abrupt, almost harsh response of Jesus is a technique we observe on his lips on a number of occasions. The purpose is apparently to test the seriousness of the inquirer's intentions (cf. Matt. 15:25; John 3:3). The same type of an introduction and response can be seen in Luke 12:13–14 where the inquirer begins with a title and is spoken to in a somewhat harsh manner. This forthright challenge to the seriousness of the questioner's intentions thus seems to be the best understanding of Jesus' answer. Bailey, Kenneth E., *Poet & Peasant and Through Peasant Eyes: A Literary-Cultural Approach to the Parables in Luke*, Combined Edition., vol. 2 (Grand Rapids, MI: William B. Eerdmans Publishing Company, 1983), 162.

Scripture. Jesus is referring to the mass of people, of all mankind, and these people must do *something*, unless... We do not yet know what needs to be accomplished. At this point in the sentence all Jesus says is that something must happen to a person, before something else must happen. But what? "Unless a man is born again." The words "born again" are literally translated "born from above." The Greek phrase is ἐὰν μή τις γεννηθῇ ἄνωθεν. It is a peculiar word (ἄνωθεν) in Greek used for the wording, "from above." Some make note about the language used, whether Jesus was speaking in Aramaic or in Greek in this conversation; though, we are sure that the Jews at this time were speaking Aramaic as their common language. Yet, word choice is important in the way the translation is taken. The question that arises in Nicodemus' mind is perplexing. Truly, it could be *more* perplexing as Jesus was speaking in Aramaic,[6] but the point here is that Nicodemus is confused at the outset. We see the Greek translation of the words Jesus uses having a spiritual application instead of a physical one. Christ moves immediately to a question of the heart, instead of placating Nicodemus in his "I saw...so it must

---

[6] By the time the Jews left exile in Babylon, and their descendants returned to Judea, their everyday language was Aramaic. Bailey rightly says, "As centuries passed, synagogues were built and in them the Scriptures were read in Hebrew and translated orally into Aramaic so that people could understand the readings." Bailey, Kenneth E. *Jesus through Middle Eastern Eyes: Cultural Studies in the Gospels,* (Downers Grove, IL: IVP Academic, 2008), 310.

be true" mentality. Christ moves the conversation by way of riddle. Men are born once, but now they must be born again. This is a strange idea to what Nicodemus would have initially understood, or what he was trying to initially convey to Christ in his response. Christ says that unless people are born again, then something else follows in the negative. *"Unless a man is born again he cannot..." There is a prerequisite for doing something here.* Men must be born again or they "cannot" do something. Jesus is drawing the motherly picture of God from the Old Testament who begets people. Giving birth is something women do. He draws from, "Of the Rock that begat thee thou art unmindful, and hast forgotten God that formed thee," (Deut. 32:18). God must give birth to these people by the supernatural agency of the Holy Spirit. "Cannot" is literally οὐ δύναται, "having no power," where we get our word *dynamite* from. The person being beget by God, has no power to do this "thing" and Jesus is describing what it means to be born from above or born again; this means he is spiritually renewed, or as commonly stated in basic Christian theology, "regenerated." Let's finish the whole sentence, "Unless a man is born again he cannot see the kingdom of heaven." Many people mistranslate this verse to mean, "Unless a man is first saved by accepting the Gospel, then he cannot enter into heaven when he dies." But this is a misinterpretation, and a reading into the text. Jesus means something completely different here.

The word "see" is not the Greek word "βλέπομεν," (i.e. we see something) which could have yielded the translation, "see with the eyes," if that is what Jesus used. *Blepow* means to physically see something with human vision, like Nicodemus *saw* Christ perform miracles. If this was the word, then the translation may be, "Unless a man is born again he cannot see with his eyes the kingdom of heaven when he gets to heaven," which then may refer to *entering* into heaven. But this would further confuse Nicodemus because seeing heaven and being born again, taken at face value, would be a riddle on top of a riddle. Jesus does not use the word "blepow" but rather a derivative of "oraow," which is "ieadien," (ἰδεῖν) meaning "to see." Are you confused? See is see right? Not really. This *seeing* here is different than the physical sight the crowd saw as in John 2:23 where the word "see" is translated as "observe and behold" by the Greek θεωροῦντες. Here, Jesus does not mean for Nicodemus to go on "seeing" in the same way the people "saw" his miracles and committed themselves to him.[7] He wants to correct Nicodemus' thinking about what it means to really see. *Seeing here in John 3:3 is not seeing*

---

[7] θεωρέω is the Greek equivalent of see, look at, observe, perceive Matt. 27:55; Mark 12:41; Luke 14:29; John 12:45; 14:17; 20:12; Acts 7:56; 9:7; 17:22; it can also mean "view" Matt. 28:1; catch sight of, notice Mark 3:11.

with the eyes, but rather, literally, "to perceive, or spiritually understand." It is as if someone said to you, "O, I see what you are saying." So the verse would be more accurately translated this way: *Unless a person is first saved by being born again by the Spirit, he cannot spiritually understand anything about the Kingdom of God.*

When Jesus says this, Nicodemus does not understand his words. This demonstrates *the case in point* – since Nicodemus is not saved, he cannot spiritually perceive Jesus' meaning, and the voice of the Shepherd is not heard.[8] Next, Nicodemus thinks Christ is referring to physical birth and asks how a man can be born again physically, a second time, picking up on Jesus' use of the idea of God begetting someone.[9] "Nicodemus saith unto him, How can a man be born when he is old? can he enter the second time into his mother's womb, and be born?" (John 3:4). The Pharisee is still stuck in the physical seeing zone. He can't seem

---

[8] "My sheep hear my voice, and I know them, and they follow me. I give them eternal life, and they will never perish, and no one will snatch them out of my hand. My Father, who has given them to me, is greater than all, and no one is able to snatch them out of the Father's hand. I and the Father are one," (John 10:27-30).

[9] The Psalmist says, "Surely I have behaved and quieted myself, as a child that is weaned of his mother: my soul is even as a weaned child," (Psa. 131:2), speaking of his relationship with God. And God is compared to a mother who remembers her child in Isa. 49:15, "Can a woman forget her sucking child, that she should not have compassion on the son of her womb? yea, they may forget, yet will I not forget thee."

to shake it. His preconceived notions about seeing is believing is hindering his understanding because his mind is darkened at this point in its total depravity. Nicodemus' sinful nature is blinding him. *He cannot "see" what Jesus is saying.*

Jesus clarifies the new question since it is helpful to his agenda by explanation, "Unless a man is born of water and the Spirit he cannot enter the kingdom of God." The "water" is physical birth.[10] Jesus is now saying, "Unless a man is born physically, (Jesus acquiesces to Nicodemus' here *via* physical birth), and is born spiritually from above by the Holy Spirit, he cannot enter the Kingdom of God." Man, unless is he saved by the Spirit of God, (big "S" for "Spirit" in the verse) will not be able to do two things: 1) he cannot spiritually perceive the Kingdom, and 2) he cannot ultimately enter the Kingdom.[11] Jesus then explains exactly what he means. He says, "That which is born of flesh is flesh and that which is born of Spirit is spirit." Flesh (man's

---

[10] Some believe this might be a reference to baptism that is associated with salvation, but that stretches the text and disregards Nicodemus' last statement. It does not consider the context at all, and does not take into consideration Jesus' teaching of being beget by God, and Nicodemus' misunderstanding that it does not refer to physical birth, having a spiritual application to the overarching theme as outlined by the Old Testament.

[11] Some believe Jesus is speaking about baptism when he speaks about water. But this stretch does not take into consideration the complete context of Jesus' repair to Nicodemus' poor theological ideas.

natural composition and spiritual nature) only gives birth to flesh. Flesh does not give birth to spirit. Only the Holy Spirit, big "S," gives birth to man's spirit, little "s". Flesh, or human nature, does not have the capacity to give birth to spiritual things. Only the motherly work of the Holy Spirit of God can "born someone again" from above.[12]

Jesus then states, "Do not marvel that I said to you, "You must be born again." The wind blows where it wishes, and you hear the sound of it, but cannot tell where it comes from or where it goes. So is everyone who is born of the Spirit." Jesus demonstrates *by analogy* to Nicodemus that the Spirit of God is sovereign over the salvation of those he chooses to save (in the same way that people do not have a say over their physical birth when they are born). It's something marvelous, but not unbelievable. Salvation and religion are not about "seeing things" that seem to point us in a Godward direction. Outwardly seeing Christ perform miracles is *not* salvific. Salvation is of the Spirit, and it is an internal operation of the Spirit on the heart to those the Spirit chooses to give birth to. The Spirit acts like the wind, for all intents and purposes, for the wind is something Nicodemus can't see, and the wind blows wherever it wants. The Spirit, like the wind, blows, "where it wishes." So the Spirit blows on whom he wishes to save,

---

[12] *cf.* Genesis 6:5; Jeremiah 17:9; Romans 3:10ff; 1 Cor. 2:1ff.

and then "borns them again," or more literally, "borns them from above," *i.e.* gives birth to them at his sovereign will. This reality of the Spirit's process is emphasized when Christ says, "So is *everyone* who is born of the Spirit." If a person is born again, they are born again by the Spirit's work. Nicodemus cannot believe such a thing is true. He says, "how can these things be?" His disbelief shows his inability to *really* see, or perceive spiritual things, as Jesus has been explaining all along.

Next, we find the completion of the dialogue portion of this chapter in verse 10. "Jesus answered and said to him, "Are you the teacher of Israel and you do not understand these things?"" Jesus *rebukes* Nicodemus and tells him that people who are spiritual teachers and rulers of God's chosen nation should know basic concepts concerning the welfare and salvation of the people, who live before a righteous and holy God, where this God requires men to be perfect.[13] Nicodemus should be intimately aware of concepts as simple as salvation if he is a true teacher of Israel; but Nicodemus was not. Salvation is a matter of the heart, not a matter of *sight*. *Outward conformity to religious ideas is not saving faith*. Miracles *may* lead someone to the Savior, they will certainly generate interest, but they do not lead a person into a saving relationship with God. That work is accomplished only by the motherly work of the Spirit of

---

[13] "Thou shalt be perfect with the LORD thy God," (Deut. 18:13).

God who births people of his own accord. John Calvin says on this verse, "As Christ sees that he is spending his time and pains to no purpose in teaching so proud a man, he begins to reprove him sharply. And certainly such persons will never make any progress, until the wicked confidence, with which they are puffed up, be removed. But, still, Nicodemus, with all his magisterial haughtiness, exposes himself to ridicule by more than childish hesitation about the first principles. Such hesitation, certainly, is base and shameful. For what religion have we, what knowledge of God, what rule of living well, what hope of eternal life, if we do not believe that man is renewed by the Spirit of God?"[14]

The theological word given to the sovereign power of the Spirit over the initial aspect of changing a person's heart during salvation, or giving them a new birth, is called, "regeneration." The Apostle Paul uses this word in Titus 3:5, "He saved us, not because of works done by us in righteousness, but according to his own mercy, by the washing of regeneration and renewal of the Holy Spirit."[15] Being "born again" is a Bible concept, and *regeneration* is a bible word (the Greek is παλιγγενεσία). It is a theologically-packed word which means, "The Spirit sovereignly blows on those whom he

---

[14] See Calvin's commentary on John 3:10, Calvin, John, *Commentary on the Gospel according to John*, Volume 1, (Bellingham, WA: Logos Bible Software, 2010), 117.
[15] παλιγγενεσία, (*paliggenesia*), meaning *born again*.

John 3:16

chooses to save, changes their heart to work a righteousness ability in them, applies the blood of Christ on them and gives them the new capacity to perceive those spiritual things they could not see before."[16] Regeneration, as a key doctrine for understanding the complete dependence of man upon Christ and his work of redemption, is a very important biblical concept all through the Old Testament, and essential in understanding salvation.[17] They are so important, that

---

[16] The blessings of the Spirit of God are only given to men when they are regenerated. They do not obtain any measure of grace unless they are regenerated and have been given saving faith. Regeneration does not come through natural revelation but by the sovereign operation of the Spirit. The 1647 Westminster Confession of Faith, 10:1, says the Spirit works on the heart of men, "enlightening their minds spiritually and savingly to understand the things of God, taking away their heart of stone, and giving unto them a heart of flesh; renewing their wills, and, by his almighty power, determining them to that which is good." See John 5:25; Eph. 1:18-20; 2 Tim. 1:8-9; Titus. 3:4-5; Eph. 2:4-5, 7-9; Rom. 9:11; 2 Cor. 5:20; 6:1-2; John 6:44; 2 Thess. 2:13-14; Acts 26:18; 1 Cor. 2:10, 12; Ezek. 11:19; 36:26-27; John 6:45; Eph. 2:5; Phil. 2:13; Deut. 30:6.

[17] It is absolutely necessary that regeneration takes place in order for a man to be released from his fallen and depraved state to the Kingdom of God. Christ, in John 3, rests upon the reality that man is *so* depraved and fallen that his spiritual birth must take place first before he ever perceives or understands of the spiritual realities of the kingdom of heaven (John 3:3, 5). In this way, the Spirit's work is crucially important in delivering and changing the heart of these men so that they may believe in the Lord Jesus Christ and be saved. This event, that *spiritual change*, is impossible with men, and only possible with God. Without a manifestly true change on the mind of the person by God, they cannot believe, nor experience any deep significant trust in or on Christ. No unregenerate man, then, can *see* the Kingdom of God unless *God wills* he should see it and converts him to be able to see it by giving birth to him, again, now from a spiritual point of view as it pertains to the fall. From all this, it is

Christ rebuked a teacher of Israel for not knowing the basics of salvation in this way. Nicodemus should have been able to glean this truth about being born again by the Spirit's work as something *fundamental* to the Hebrew Bible, *i.e.* the Old Testament. That means regeneration, or being born from above, is a concept God taught his people in the Old Testament. Consider some Old Testament verses Nicodemus should have been familiar with. "But my servant Caleb, because he has a different spirit and has followed me fully, I will bring into the land into which he went, and his descendants shall possess it," (Num. 14:24). Where did Caleb's *different spirit* come from? Even more blatantly, God says in Ezekiel, "I will remove the heart of stone from their flesh and give them a heart of flesh," (Ezek. 11:19). Again, "A new heart also will I give you, and a new spirit will I put within you: and I will take away the stony heart out of your flesh, and I will give you an heart of flesh," (Ezek. 36:26).

    How does regeneration work? Remember, Jesus would not commit himself to the crowd because he knew what was in the heart of men. Man is sinful, and cannot believe or perceive anything about the kingdom of God while in a sinful state. The Spirit must arrest his

---

manifest that redemption itself proceeds on the principle that God must allow admission to his kingdom *first*, and to apply a spiritual principle that quickens the soul to life.

heart, blow on him and change his heart in the process of giving birth to a, "spirit." The person is then able to believe and *perceive* the kingdom, and does so *because* of the work of the Spirit. And we know, since there is a hell, that the Spirit does not regenerate *all* people. He chooses to regenerate some and passes by others. He blows as the wind; where he blows and when he blows is a mystery to us. This would have been a radical thought to Nicodemus who thought that *being a Jew* was in fact *being chosen* by God. Now he is being corrected by Christ who demonstrates the Spirit's sovereignty in saving those he chooses, as a mother gives birth to children who have no say in their own birth. *Practically speaking, regeneration may be seen as the time when the Spirit of God, on an unsaved person, removes the heart of stone he had been born with because of his sinful nature on account of the fall, and replaces it with a heart of flesh so that he will respond positively to the Gospel which he could not understand before.* In this way, we see that according to Jesus Christ, regeneration *precedes* faith.

The church today has salvation backwards. How is this so? Follow this example. Christians today believe that a person attends church, hears the evangelistic message, thinks about it, and then decides whether or not to believe it and follow Jesus. He hears first, decides second, and then is born again, third. But this is not what Jesus says to Nicodemus. Jesus asserts that a man must first be born again before he can spiritually perceive, or understand, *anything* about the Kingdom of heaven. He comes to church hears the message and understands or perceives nothing about it because he is spiritually dead.[18] Being spiritually dead does not mean he is "sort of spiritually alive." He is alive physically, but he is a spiritual corpse for all intents and purposes as it relates to God's spiritual Kingdom. There is no spiritual life in him *at all.* The Spirit must quicken his heart and mind by giving birth to his dead spirit and renewing his heart to beat after God.[19] God takes out the heart of stone and puts in a heart of flesh. The dead heart of all sinners can do nothing but sit as a heart of stone, with no beating pulse, with no perception of spiritual good. "Because the carnal mind is enmity against God: for it is

---

[18] The natural, or unrenewed man, (one who has not been born of the Spirit) is entirely unable of himself to do anything good in the sight of God. "...who were dead in trespasses and sins..." (Eph. 2:1). "Adam having sinned by eating, the threatening of death was fulfilled; because upon his fault his soul was spiritually dead, and his body thenceforth liable to natural death, and to all miseries, as fore-runners thereof; God reprieved him and spared the full execution of the sentence, to commend his abundant mercy and patience in giving him both space and occasion of repentance, (2 Peter 3; Rom. 2:4)." Wilson, Thomas, *Theological Rules, to Guide Us in the Understanding and Practice of Holy Scriptures,* (London: Edw. Griffin, 1615) 27-28.

[19] "And you were dead in the trespasses and sins in which you once walked, following the course of this world, following the prince of the power of the air, the spirit that is now at work in the sons of disobedience," (Eph. 2:1-2). Dead is spiritually *dead.*

not subject to the law of God, neither indeed can be," (Rom. 8:7). Unless the Spirit of God arrests his heart and "borns him from above," he will not understand the Kingdom of God, nor will he enter into it no matter how many times he hears the Gospel, or how many times he sees Jesus perform miracles. In both seeing and hearing, the prophecy of Isaiah is fulfilled in them, "And in them is fulfilled the prophecy of Esaias, which saith, By hearing ye shall hear, and shall not understand; and seeing ye shall see, and shall not perceive," (Matt. 13:14). The Spirit must work the ability and tool which illicit *belief* in him by regenerating his heart so that he has new spiritual eyes and new spiritual ears. The dead heart is removed and a living heart, one born of God, is put in its place. "And the LORD thy God will circumcise thine heart, and the heart of thy seed, to love the LORD thy God with all thine heart, and with all thy soul, that thou mayest live," (Deut. 30:6).

In the *basics of salvation,* the church has reversed the order of salvation. Nicodemus missed the manner of true salvation altogether, as so many ministers do today! How could he be Israel's teacher, and miss the very basics of what constitutes eternal salvation and regeneration for those looking to go to heaven? Most of Christendom believes that it depends *on man* rather than on the sovereign act of the Spirit of God who applies the blood of Christ's covenant to those whom he chooses to blow on and give birth to. Why do most pastors teach an erroneous view of salvation in today's Christian climate? They do this because they disregard Jesus' words to Nicodemus (they ignore the text), and jump right to John 3:16 with preconceived notions.

Study Questions for Part 3

1. Is there a difference between the terms "born from above" and "born again?" Why or why not is this important?

2. Does *born again* mean *saved?* What does it mean to be saved?

3. What is regeneration?

4. What are some important theological implications concerning the sinful nature of man since regeneration precedes saving faith?

5. As a teacher of the Jews, what would Nicodemus have required of a full-born Jew to do in order to be considered one of the chosen people of God?

6. What does Jesus set on men as a prerequisite for them to be one of the chosen people of God?

Part 4:
John 3:11-15

"Verily, verily, I say unto thee, We speak that we do know, and testify that we have seen; and ye receive not our witness," (John 3:11).

Now the tide turns. The dialogue finishes with a rebuke of the ignorant "pastor" or "ruler" of God's people, who now must *unlearn* most everything he thought he knew. And here, Jesus preaches to him, instructing him on vital truths concerning the message the Son of Man came to bring the world. The dialogue has ended and Jesus turns to instructing the one who should have been instructed in such things all along.

"We know." A book could be written on this phrase alone based on the two contexts we must deal with in this passage. The "we know" that Nicodemus stated, is a knowledge of seeing with the eyes, making wrong conclusions based on a depraved heart, and is a misinterpretation of everything he has ever learned as a guide to God's church. Jesus' "we know" in this verse stems from close communion, intimate communion with the Father for all eternity. It is a radically different knowledge based not only on close communion, but intimate interaction.

Who is the "we" of "we know?" In relationship to the coming of the Kingdom, the testification of that kingdom was by divine right of the Christ as God's covenant Mediator. The word "testify" here is also used of John the Baptist, testifying of the *One* to come. The "we" is not Jesus saying "Me and the Old Testament witness," but the outward testifying of the coming of the Kingdom of God by the forerunner John the Baptist (the Elijah to his Elisha), and his testifying of the truth in being the Word of God, the Logos, come down from heaven (consider John 3:13).

The people that have heard John the Baptist preach about the Kingdom, and those that have heard and seen Jesus' preaching and miracles "do not accept" their testimony. The reason is simple; darkened minds hate God's kingdom (John 7:7, 15:18; 1 John 3:13).[1] They hate the truth, and they cannot accept or receive the truth unless the Spirit gives them a regenerated heart to believe the message the Son of Man delivered from above to fallen humanity below.[2] Jesus continues, "If I have told you earthly things, and ye believe not, how shall ye

---

[1] People *hate* God and his Law as unconverted souls. Exodus 20:5; Deut. 5:9; Proverbs 8:36; "...haters of God," (Rom. 1:30).

[2] Fallen men do not understand that which is *good*. Acts 16:14 says, "Now a certain woman named Lydia heard us. She was a seller of purple from the city of Thyatira, who worshiped God. The Lord opened her heart to heed the things spoken by Paul." Since men do not understand that which is good, the Lord must *open* their heart to receive the truth, without which, they will not and do not receive it.

believe, if I tell you of heavenly things?" (John 3:12). Things that occur while we are here on earth, like regeneration, are essential for a true relationship with the Father. If those things are rejected as *false*, as the Pharisees and Sanhedrin rejected such things time and time again all through the Gospels and Acts, then how will they understand anything that Christ may teach them concerning things that occur in heaven? In other words, if the basics of the Spirit's power in regeneration is rejected, how will you, Nicodemus, understand anything I teach you about the salvation of people from every tribe tongue and nation, (*cf.* John 3:16)? To bring this more clearly home, if Christians today reject the orthodox position and historical understanding of John 3:1-10 (and they often do) how will they understand of heavenly things contained in John 3:16? Jesus continues, "And no man hath ascended up to heaven, but he that came down from heaven, even the Son of man which is in heaven," (John 3:13). If Christ is going to preach to Nicodemus about first-hand knowledge of heavenly things, a prerequisite is to have that first-hand knowledge of having been in heaven and come down to earth to explain them to ignorant Pharisees. No man on earth has ever gone up into heaven, then come back to teach the church about heavenly things. Instead, Christ focuses on his work as the Son of Man who came from heaven to earth to redeem his people.

The phrase "Son of Man" is another one of those phrases that could fill a few thousand books. It is a very misunderstood phrase and designation of the Christ. To many people, "Son of Man," *seems* to have linked to it, at face value, the meek human Jesus who is the suffering servant. This is not the case at all. The term is used in the Old Testament, one which Nicodemus should be familiar with, and ought to prick him in the inner recesses of his heart. It is the glorious, majestic description of God's court room Judge who opens the books and judges all men. He is the one who rides the clouds of the Shekinah glory of God, and holds the power of judgment in his hands. It is conveyed through the prophets, but graphically depicted in Daniel and in Revelation. "I saw in the night visions, and, behold, one like the Son of man came with the clouds of heaven, and came to the Ancient of days, and they brought him near before him. And there was given him dominion, and glory, and a kingdom, that all people, nations, and languages, should serve him: his dominion is an everlasting dominion, which shall not pass away, and his kingdom that which shall not be destroyed," (Dan. 7:13-14).[3] And then Revelation 1:13-18, "And in the midst of

---

[3] The stress is on verse 13 of John 3, "No one has ascended to heaven but He who came down from heaven, that is, the Son of Man who is in heaven," (John 3:13). The phrase "Son of Man" is the intended focus, which means, in order to understand John 3, the Old Testament must be considered. Little did Nicodemus know with

the seven candlesticks one like unto the Son of man, clothed with a garment down to the foot, and girt about the paps with a golden girdle. His head and his hairs were white like wool, as white as snow; and his eyes were as a flame of fire; And his feet like unto fine brass, as if they burned in a furnace; and his voice as the sound of many waters. And he had in his right hand seven stars: and out of his mouth went a sharp two- edged sword: and his countenance was as the sun shineth in his strength. And when I saw him, I fell at his feet as dead. And he laid his right hand upon me, saying unto me, Fear not; I am the first and the last: I am he that liveth, and was dead; and, behold, I am alive for evermore, Amen; and have the keys of hell and of death," (Rev. 1:13-18).

The section in Daniel demonstrates the prequel to the passage in Revelation. They depict the same occurrence of events, by the same person, the Son of Man. Try to imagine vividly what Nicodemus is *hearing*. Jesus is claiming the title of the Son of Man, the judgment title that the Ancient of Days gives him to judge and with sovereign dominion and power over all nations, tribes and people. This is an important concept once John 3:16 is reached. Nicodemus *has* read Daniel, but now he was being lectured from the One who has come down from heaven, who has God's glory and utter

---

whom he was speaking, for his sight, at this point, is deceiving him in more ways than one.

dominion, and will judge all men for all time; he is being lectured by the one who is he that Nicodemus has read about in Daniel. At this point, I would imagine Nicodemus being *mortally frightened*, and yet, still *utterly* confused. Even with a cursory knowledge of the Hebrew Scriptures, connecting the dots on who Christ is at this point, with Christ speaking to him, rebuking him, and teaching him, would have been more than a man could bear. But we have no further notes on the disposition or reaction of Nicodemus; such is only speculation.

The center of this whole chapter focuses on God's redemptive plan for mankind. It centers on being born again, and seeing or perceiving eternal life as given by the Spirit, based on God's plan. Jesus then explains the Old Testament again to Nicodemus, "And as Moses lifted up the serpent in the wilderness, even so must the Son of man be lifted up: That whosoever believeth in him should not perish, but have eternal life," (John 3:14-15). Jesus refers to his copy of the Scriptures. Nicodemus should be well aware of the narrative of Moses and the brass serpent. In Numbers 21 Moses is instructed by God to fashion a serpent in the wilderness made of brass. The people of God had been rebellious and God had sent a plague of fiery serpents to bite and kill unbelievers. The remedy was simple, *look* on the brass serpent that they lifted up in the midst of the people on a tall pole. Anyone who was bitten that looked to the remedy God had sovereignly provided would be made well. It does not take much to understand Jesus' connection and quotation of this passage of Scripture in John 3.

The link between the Numbers 21 narrative and John 3 explains God's manner of sovereign redemption. In Numbers 21, the people sinned and the result is that *death* should be the punishment. But, graciously, even though the people sinned, God gave them a remedy for sin. God was not obliged, nor did he have to fashion anything for the Israelites. He could have justly allowed them all to perish. But God's sovereign and gracious plan of redemption was bigger than the sin of the people. In public view, *God's means of redemption was to be lifted up and believed on by faith, i.e. seen with the perceptive eyes of faith.* In our current context, Jesus has already explained where such believing comes from – the sovereignty of the Spirit blowing on individuals to give them hearts of flesh likened to a mother giving birth to her children. But Christ instructs Nicodemus that the Son of Man *must be lifted up.*[4] This may have seemed to

---

[4] Being "lifted up" is seen in two ways, and the first is by death, and the second is by exaltation after death, to resurrection, and ascension. "And as Moses lifted up the serpent in the wilderness, even so must the Son of Man be lifted up," (John 3:14). "Now it came to pass, when Jesus had finished all these sayings, that He said to His disciples, "You know that after two days is the Passover, and the Son of Man will be delivered up to be crucified,"" (Matt. 26:1-2). Such an infinite sacrifice for the Son of Man to make, he is hailed as worthy to receive power and riches and wisdom, and strength and

be a cryptic idea given to Nicodemus at the time, but in light of the historical narrative of Christ's passion in the Gospels, we know what it means because *we fill in* (perceptually) the information based on the historical narrative that we already have. The Son of Man, the glorious Judge who has all power and dominion over all people, tribes and nations, must be sacrificed to atone for the sin of his people. Christ tells Nicodemus that whoever believes this, will have eternal life.

Christ has moved from being born again and seeing the kingdom of heaven, (spiritually perceiving), to *having* eternal life based on *believing* the heavenly truths of the redemption made possible by the Son of Man after having been born again. The Spirit gives men

---

honor and glory and blessing, (Rev. 5:12). In this crucifixion God accepted the sacrifice of the Son of Man as the merit necessary in value and price by which any man may be perfectly reconciled to God. The Son of Man provides atonement, a substitution; a lamb for a life. "The Lord of glory was crucified;" and, "God purchased the church with his own blood," (1 Cor. 2:8; Acts 20:28). The Son of Man was murdered, brutally. He was beaten within inches of his human life, stripped naked, abandoned by his disciples, forced to walk naked publicly to carry his cross to the place of execution, nailed to it, scoffed at by the religious leaders of the day, and scoffed at by the worst among thieves, and then was given over to death being abandoned by the Father and his curse. "Cursed is everyone who hangs on a tree." The Son of Man willingly laid down his life to allow the worst crime in history, in the worst way, to take place. "Christ, being delivered by the determinate counsel and foreknowledge of God, you have taken, and by wicked hands have crucified and slain," (Acts 2:23). He must be killed, and he must be lifted up. He died, was buried in a tomb, and again was lifted up in resurrection.

the ability to believe; and when the truth of the Gospel message of the Son of Man being lifted up in public view due to the sacrifice of himself for sin is believed, men are then saved. They are not simply saved in the Anti-type of the serpent lifted up on a pole for mortal healing, but the healing that the Son of Man brings from heaven is eternal and everlasting. As the serpent in the wilderness was lifted up in public view, so too the Son of Man is lifted up for the redemption of his people. But the mere fact of "lifting" up is *not saving everyone* as a result of this lifting up. In other words, Jesus does not save everyone *as he is* lifted up on the cross. *The mere act of lifting up the Son of Man in public view does not save the world. Only those who believe are saved.* Only those who have the capacity of believing can be saved. And they must, (and they will), look to the Son of Man lifted up and believe on him to have everlasting life.[5] In Nicodemus' eyes, this would be the opposite of seeing

---

[5] When faith springs from a redeemed heart it is called a "reflex act." Most Christians have never even heard of this. A doctor often takes that little reflex hammer and taps one's knee to make sure the knee has a proper *reflex*. The connection of the hammer to the knee elicits that response every time if the knee is working correctly. When the knee is hit, it kicks out by reflex. Love to God *is a reflex act* by the pardoned soul due to God's love and salvation in Christ to them first. Sinners, that have been *born again* act with this reflex when they believe the Gospel by faith, because of what Christ has done, and what the Spirit has done in applying the work of Christ to the soul. God gives them a *new birth* by the Spirit, and then their lives take on *new perspectives.* God's love in them is exercised against all that God hates. If the soul has not been changed, it remains bound in sin.

miracles. It would be the killing of the Son of Man, and unthinkable action, or impossible even, knowing that such a one is the Shekinah of God's radiance and dominion. How does one kill God?

Study Questions for Part 4

1. Jesus and John the Baptist testified about the coming of the Kingdom; why did the people not believe them?

2. What is the most striking similarity between the brass serpent and Christ's use of that narrative in John 3?

3. What does it mean for Christ to be the Son of Man as depicted in Daniel 7?

4. Explain how seeing the brass serpent was *not* the same as Nicodemus' seeing of Christ's miracles.

5. What does it mean *to be obliged* to do something?

6. Why was God *not* obliged to save the Israelites *via* a brass serpent in the wilderness?

Part 5:
John 3:16

"For God so loved the world, that he gave his only begotten Son, that whosoever believeth in him should not perish, but have everlasting life," (John 3:16).

We have come, rather quickly, to John 3:16. Be reminded, most Christians skip the first 45 pages of this work to jump to this point and hope their view lines up with what is about to be said concerning Christ's most historically famous Bible instruction. We will be getting technical with some of the words and phrases here, but this is essential to understand the passage. The footnotes I have in this section are much more extensive than in other sections and will aid the reader with extra information.

As we said in the beginning of this little book, John 3:16 is often utilized out of the context of Jesus' discussion in teaching Nicodemus. It's often employed as a proof text for God's saving love to the entire world.[1] Some Christians believe that God intends here a general

---

[1] The word "world" is considered, for proponents of the idea of *common grace* and *the saving love of God to all men*, to mean "all people for all time." It would *have* to be. Would this then include those already assigned to hell? It would *have* to be. But that illogically does not fit their judgment of already being in hell, or Jesus' directions to Nicodemus.

"saving" love to all men. Forcing John 3:16 to mean a "general love" ignores the passage entirely. It does what Nicodemus was doing, misunderstanding God's word on a very basic level even amidst Jesus' didactic teaching to the contrary. Neither the context, nor the grammar, nor the specific use of the words "so" and "gave," allow for a *general love* to *all* men.² Hugh Latimer has stated, "God is not only a private Father, but a common Father unto the whole world, unto all the faithful, be they never so poor and miserable."³ Latimer says that the world of the faithful, and they alone, have God as their Father. That means God cannot love, with the highest love, all men for all time. First, the text reads, "For God so loved the world that He gave His only begotten Son, that whoever believes in Him should not perish but have everlasting life."⁴ The article, γὰρ, (gar), "for" denotes the

---

² R.K. McGregor Wright states, "If the verse is disputed, its meaning is no longer obvious, and it is probably time to do some homework. As we discovered with the well-known verse John 3:16, a brief look at the Greek instantly destroyed the apparently obvious Arminian meaning." Hopefully this brief look at the verse will, in hand, prove Wright as right. See *No Place for Sovereignty* (Downers Grove: InterVarsity Press, 1996), 167.

³ Latimer, Hugh, *Latimer's Sermons*, vol. 1, 332, as quoted in *The Works of Augustus Toplady*, 142. Latimer also states that, "Now it would both impeach the wisdom, and affront the dignity of Christ, as well as infinitely depreciate the value of His sacrifice to suppose that he could possibly shed his blood on the cross, for those very souls which were, at that very time, suffering for their own sins in hell." Ibid., 142.

⁴ Οὕτως γὰρ ἠγάπησεν ὁ θεὸς τὸν κόσμον, ὥστε τὸν υἱὸν αὐτοῦ τὸν μονογενῆ ἔδωκεν, ἵνα πᾶς ὁ πιστεύων εἰς αὐτὸν μὴ ἀπόληται, ἀλλ' ἔχῃ ζωὴν αἰώνιον, (John 3:16).

information previous in the conversation which Jesus is expounding to Nicodemus. Keep in mind that the immediate context refers to the brass serpent in the wilderness for those who would look upon it.[5] The larger context is on regeneration and Jesus' discourse with Nicodemus—how the Spirit, Son, and Father accomplish redemption *for* fallen men. The "for" is immediately connected with the objects of the last verse instrumentally; everyone who believes should not perish because God sent his Son for those who would believe. The "for" of the verse links the thought in the previous verse, 3:15, to verse 16. The "for" is transitive.[6] It is also to be noted that John 3:16 recalls the promise of the prologue seen in 1:12-13 and prepares the reader of the Gospel to encounter God's expanded realm of salvation, not only for the Jews, but also for the Samaritans and Gentiles in John 4:1-54.[7] This is something the Pharisee would have rejected. God will save Samaritans and Gentiles? Nicodemus would have rejected that thought in general conversation. The author of this love is God.

---

[5] Numbers 21:8, "Then The Lord said to Moses, Make a fiery serpent, and set it on a pole; and it shall be that everyone who is bitten, when he looks at it, shall live."

[6] *Transitive* refers to a verb which requires a direct object to complete its meaning. See Barclay Moon Newman and Eugene Albert Nida, *A Handbook on Paul's Letter to the Romans*, (New York: United Bible Societies, 1973), 314.

[7] Moloney, Franncis J., *Sacra Pagina*, (Collegeville: Liturgical Press, 1946), 96.

The grammar is literally, "so loved God."[8] The word, "Οὕτως" (houtos) is the emphatically[9] used "so" of the verse.[10] It is not a general love, but an emphatic love,[11] of

---

[8] Morris, Leon, *New International Commentary on the New Testament*, John (Grand Rapids: Wm. B. Eerdmans Publishing Co., 1989), 229. This is the first use of *agapaow*, used 36 more times through John's Gospel.

[9] Owen, John, *The Works of John Owen*, Volume 1, (Carlisle, PA: Banner of Truth Trust, 1995) 28. John 3:16, "God so loved the world, that he gave," *etc.*; that is, with the love of his purpose and good pleasure, his determinate will of doing good. This is distinctly ascribed to him, being laid down as the cause of sending his Son. See also Romans 9:11, 12; Ephesians 1:4, 5; 2 Thessalonians 2:13, 14; 1 John 4:8-9.

[10] Aquinas, Thomas, *Summa Theologia*, 421. Now, that the Son of God took to Himself flesh from the Virgin's womb was due to the exceeding love of God: wherefore it is said (John 3:16): "God so loved the world as to give His only-begotten Son."

[11] Even the Arminian, R.C.H. Lenski states in his *Commentary on John* (Augsburg Publishing House: Minneapolis, MN, 1943), 259-260, that the word denotes manner and degree, stressing the word "love" which is in the aorist tense attesting to an accomplished fact. He says on page 262, that the "so...that" construction with the indicative expresses the attained actual result. It is not something hypothetical but real and actual. The degree is the greatest love of God, and the result is the redemption of all those who believe. Even the word "gave" (page 264), is in the aorist tense denoting a historical past action of the Father for us.

which there is none higher than this.[12] The "so" stresses[13] the aorist tense of the verb "ἠγάπησεν" (agapasen)." "So" is an adverb in this instance, connected vitally as a preceding intensive particle to the verb "love". As an adverb, it denotes the "degree of intensity" of the verb to be stated. As is often noted, the phrase as a whole ("For God so loved the world") is a clause attached to a subordinate result clause ("that he gave."). This is important since it causes the phrase to stand on its own, except for the connection between the last verse and the word "for." The meaning, then, is quite straight forward in the Greek. Not only did God love the world, but he

---

[12] Turretin, Francis. *Institutes of Elenctic Theology*, Volume 1, (Phillipsburg, NJ: Presbyterian and Reformed Publishing Company, 1992-94), 242. Turretin states that God, in John 3:16 is electing the church. He makes the distinction between the effect and cause saying, "the effect of election cannot be called its cause," *cf.* page 352. "The love treated in John 3:16 when it is said that "God so loved the world, that he gave His only begotten son," cannot be universal towards each and every one, but special towards a few. 1) It treats of the supreme and intense love of God (a greater than which cannot be conceived) towards those for whom he gave his only begotten. This is evident both from the intensive (*epitakite*) particle *houtos* (which has great weight here) and from the thing itself. Turretin, Institutes, vol. 1, 405; Turretin was aware of Calvin's interpretation of this passage, which he makes this note on page 405, Section 30.

[13] Boettner, Lorraine, "Contradicts Universalistic Passages" in *The Reformed Doctrine of Predestination* (Phillipsburg: Presbyterian and Reformed Publishing Company, 1932), 293-294. He believes the verse pertains to all men of all kinds (Jews and Gentiles), "the intensity of God's love is made plain by the little adverb "so". But where is the often-boasted proof of it universality as to individuals?" Boettner goes on to prove that it is not to the whole world but to the elect in the whole world."

intensely loved the world which is emphatically seen in use of *houtos*.

The particular use of the word *love*, is to love something in particular or to "delight in the object."[14] The "love" spoken of here by the Savior cannot be a lesser love than that with which God loves his elect people. The aorist active indicative of "agapao" is the word so common in the Gospels for the highest form of love. It is used here as it often is in the writings of John (14:23; 17:23; 1 John 3:1; 4:10). It is used of God's love for his elect (2 Thessalonians 2:16; Romans 5:8; Ephesians 2:4).[15] If this love in John 3:16 is "so" great as to be towards the whole world, this would cause the love of God to the whole world to be *greater* than the love he has for his elect people in Christ. This would not make *any* biblical sense, and it would defeat the purpose of the statement Christ is making to this Pharisee in explaining the relationship of his words to the Scriptural Old Testament idea of salvation as it pertains to the lifting up of the Son of Man. To love everyone, in this saving way, would include those in hell, and would include people like Esau and Pharaoh, both of which God says

---

[14] Spiros Zhodiates states that the word "love" in the Greek in these, and many other instances, refers to a "delighting" in the object of the love. See Zhodiates, Spiros, *Word Study Dictionary*, (Chattanooga, TN: AMG Publishers, 1992) 65.

[15] Robertson, A.T., *Word Pictures in the New Testament*, Volume 5, (Grand Rapids: Baker Book House, 1960), 50.

he *hates* not loves.[16] Jesus says in John 15:13, "Greater love has no one than this, than to lay down one's life for his friends." If this is true, (and it is), then the love which is spoken of in John 3:16 is the greatest love.[17] So, if this is true, and no greater love can be exemplified than this love which causes Christ to lay his life down for his friends, then the "world," of necessity, would have to be universally saved since God "so loves" it. And when Christ dies on the cross, he does not make a "way" of salvation, but actually saves those for whom he died. "It is finished," does not mean, it is *partly* finished until sinful, spiritually dead men respond to my work in a way that God finds acceptable. This is *certainly* not true. It is true, though, that the love which is stated here is the greatest love God ever had, but it is for his elect.[18]

Turretin rightly states (italics are mine): The love treated in John 3:16 when it is said that "God so loved the world, that he gave his only begotten Son,"

---

[16] "Esau I have hated," (Mal. 1:3) quoted in Romans 9:13, "Jacob I loved, but Esau I hated," (Rom. 9:13).

[17] D.A. Carson rightly points out that the Greek construction behind "so loved that he gave his only begotten son" (houtos plus hoste plus the indicative instead of the infinitive) emphasizes the intensity of that love. See *The Gospel According to John* (Grand Rapids: Wm. B. Eerdman's Publishing Company, 1991), 204.

[18] Some say that stating God's love here is towards the "elect" ruins the force of the sentence. Yet, it seems that the construction in the Greek not only does not ruin it for the elect, but amply strengthens it. On this passage, the Puritan John Howe states, "could the love of God be under restraint? And I say, no it could not." Frederick Wesley and A.H. Davis, eds., The Works of Rev. John Howe (London, 1832), 94. I would agree with Howe on this.

cannot be universal towards each and every one, but special towards a few. (1) It treats of the supreme and immense love of God[19] (a greater than which is not and cannot be conceived) to those he gave his only begotten. This is evident both from the intensive (*epitatike*) particle *houtos* (which has great weight here) and from the thing itself. For no one can have a greater love than to lay down his life for his friends (John 15:13), so no greater love can be found than that by which God (when men were yet enemies) delivered his own Son to death for them...on the elect alone, he bestows all things with Christ.[20] The object of the love is "τὸν κόσμον" (ton

---

[19] Raymond E. Brown states, "the classical use of this construction is for the purpose of stressing the reality of the result." *The Gospel According to John*, (Garden City: Doubleday & Co., 1966), 134.

[20] Turretin, *Institutes*, Volume 1, 405. Turretin goes on to say, "(3) Therefore the end of that love which God intends is the salvation of those whom he pursues with such love; hence he adds, "For God sent not his son into the world to condemn the world, but that the world through him might be saved" (John 3:17). If therefore God sent Christ for that end (that through him the world might be saved), he must either have failed of his end or the world must be necessarily saved in fact. However, it is certain that not the whole world, but only the chosen out of the world are saved; therefore, to them properly this love has reference. Nor can it be conceived if a universal love is here understood, how such and so great love (which is by far the cause of the greatest and most excellent good, *viz.*, the mission of Christ) can consist with the hatred of innumerable persons whom he willed to pass by and ordain to damnation (to whom he never has revealed either his Son or willed to bestow faith, without which it is set forth in vain). Nor can it be conceived how this love of God can be so greatly commended here which yet remains void and inefficacious on account of the defect of subjective grace, which God has determined to deny."

John 3:16

cosmon,[21] the world). John Gill states that the Persic version translates the word "world" as "men", which, in this case may be fitting though not necessary.[22] John

---

[21] Instances of this can be found in the following set *Puritan Sermons* 1659-1689 (Wheaton: Richard Owen Roberts Publishers, 1981). William Whitaker, Puritan Sermons, vol. 1, 513; vol. 5, 213; Thomas Vincent, Puritan Sermons, vol. 2, 630; Thomas Doolittle, Puritan Sermons, vol. 4, 8. "The Spirit of God doth sanctify some that they may be partakers of the eternal inheritance of the saints in light." Samuel Annesley, Puritan Sermons, vol. 5, 187. He places John 3:16 as the covenant of grace made with sinners"; John Gibbon, Puritan Sermons, vol. 5, 323. He sees John 3:16 as "Jesus given to believers." Richard Fairclough, Puritan Sermons, vol. 6, 386. He links John 3:16 with Ephesians 2:8-10 inseparably together as to the elect.

[22] Gill, John, *Exposition of the Old and New Testaments*, Volume 7, (Paris: Baptist Standard Bearer, 1989), 772-773. "For God so loved the world..." The Persic version reads "men": but not every man in the world is here meant, or all the individuals of human nature; for all are not the objects of God's special love, which is here designed, as appears from the instance and evidence of it, the gift of his Son: nor is Christ God's gift to every one; for to whomsoever he gives his Son, he gives all things freely with him; which is not the case of every man. Nor is human nature here intended, in opposition to, and distinction from, the angelic nature; for though God has showed a regard to fallen men, and not to fallen angels, and has provided a Savior for the one, and not for the other; and Christ has assumed the nature of men, and not angels; yet not for the sake of all men, but the spiritual seed of Abraham; and besides, it will not be easily proved, that human nature is ever called the world: nor is the whole body of the chosen ones, as consisting of Jews and Gentiles, here designed; for though these are called the world (John 6:33, 51); and are the objects of God's special love, and to them Christ is given, and they are brought to believe in him, and shall never perish, but shall be saved with an everlasting salvation; yet rather the Gentiles particularly, and God's elect among them, are meant; who are often called "the world", and "the whole world", and "the nations of the world", as distinct from the Jews; see Romans 11:12, 15; 1 John 2:2; Luke 12:30. compared with Matthew 6:32. The Jews had the same distinction we have now, the church and the world; the former they took to themselves, and the latter they gave to all the nations

Part 5: John 3:16

Flavel rightly states, "The objects of this love, or the persons to whom the eternal Lord delivered Christ, and that is the world. This must respect the elect of God in the world, such as do, or shall actually believe, as it is exegetically expressed in the next words, 'That

---

around: hence we often meet with this distinction, Israel, and the nations of the world; on those words, "let them bring forth their witness", that they may be justified, Isaiah 43:9, says the doctors, these are Israel; "or let them hear and say it is truth", these are "the nations of the world"." And again, "the holy, blessed God said to Israel, when I judge Israel, I do not judge them as "the nations of the world", and so in a multitude of places: and it should be observed, that our Lord was now discoursing with a Jewish Rabbi, and that he is opposing a commonly received notion of theirs, that when the Messiah came, the Gentiles should have no benefit or advantage by him, only the Israelites; so far should they be from it, that, according to their sense, the most dreadful judgments, calamities, and curses, should befall them; yea, hell and eternal damnation. "There is a place (they say) the name of which is "Hadrach", Zechariah 9:1. This is the King Messiah, who is ("sharp and tender"; sharp to "the nations", and tender to "Israel." And so of the "sun of righteousness", in Malachi 4:2, they say, "there is healing for the Israelites in it: but the idolatrous nations shall be burnt by it." And that "there is mercy for Israel, but judgment for the rest of the nations." And on those words in Isaiah 21:12, "the morning cometh", and also the night, they observe, "the morning is for the righteous, and the night for the wicked; the morning is for Israel, and the night for "the nations of the world"." And again, "in the time to come (the times of the Messiah), the holy, blessed God will bring "darkness" upon "the nations", and will enlighten Israel, as it is said, Isaiah 60:2" Once more, "in the time to come, the holy, blessed God will bring the nations of the world, and will cast them into the midst of hell under the Israelites, as it is said, Isaiah 43:3." To which may be added that denunciation of theirs, "woe to the nations of the world, who perish, and they know not that they perish: in the time that the sanctuary was standing, the altar atoned for them; but now who shall atone for them?"

John 3:16

whosoever believes in him should not perish.'"[23] As John Owen states, God of his free grace, has prepared a way to redeem and save his elect, (John 3:16; Isaiah 53:6).[24] I believe it is difficult to translate the verse in any other fashion without entering into great theological problems.[25] The *world* cannot mean all men

---

[23] Flavel, John, *The Works of John Flavel*, Volume 1, (Carlisle, Banner of Truth Trust: 1995) 63.

[24] See Owen's "Catechism: Of the Incarnation of Christ," *Works*, Volume 12, 283ff.

[25] Turretin, *Institutes*, Volume 1, 407. "The universal particles which often occur here are not always employed in their whole extent, but sometimes more broadly, sometimes more strictly, according to the subject matter. Sometimes they denote the whole of the nations in distinction to the Old Testament economy where salvation was only of the Jews. Thus, the passage of Paul must be explained when he says that "God hath concluded them all in unbelief, that he might have mercy upon all" (Romans 11:32). This ought not to be referred to each and every one, but only to the peoples of whom he treats-to teach that the Jews as well as Gentiles were concluded in unbelief that the mercy of God might be exercised towards both distributively, Jews as well as Gentiles. This is evident from the very connection of the words (Romans 11:30-31). Thus, we understand his words, "Whosoever believeth shall not be ashamed, for there is no difference between the Jew and the Greek; for the same Lord over all, is rich unto all that call upon him" (Romans 10:11-12). Here also belongs the passage: "Of a truth I perceive that God is no respecter of persons: but in every nation he that feareth him, is accepted with him" (Acts 10:34-35). (2) Sometimes the universality of conditions and states is designated in opposition to worldly polities. Thus, distinctions are made between slaves and the free, the poor and the rich, men and women, the noble and the ignoble. But in the dispensation of grace, God attends to no such thing, nor accepts the person, but calls to communion with him indiscriminately all of whatever state and condition and sex. Thus, we understand the place where "the grace that bringeth salvation" is said to "have appeared to all men" (Titus 2:11-12), *i.e.,* to everyone of whatever condition they may be, whether masters or servants. For of these he was speaking in the preceding verse, and after having exhorted

indiscriminately for all time. God's love does not extend to all men for all time, even those who were presently in hell while Jesus was speaking to Nicodemus.

The word "world" cannot be loosely translated as meaning every one for all time, including those who have already perished. No one would grant that it includes all men in hell, or those who had previously been in hell at the time of the crucifixion, or refer to

---

masters to treat their servants kindly, he immediately adds "For the grace that bringeth salvation hath appeared to all," i.e., to them as well as to you. Also "in Christ there is neither circumcision nor uncircumcision, bond nor free, Barbarian nor Scythian; but Christ is all, and in all" (Colossians 3:11) not in each and every individual, but in all indiscriminately of whatever order, sex, nation and condition. (3) Sometimes the whole of believers and the world of the elect (as opposed to the world of the reprobate and unbelievers) is understood. Thus, all are said "to live in Christ just as in Adam all die" (1 Corinthians 15:22). Not that there is the same latitude of those living as those dying, for many more die in Adam than are saved in Christ. With regard to the whole of believers, as many as perish and die, die in Adam; so as many as are made alive, are made alive in Christ. For these two heads are compared with each other, not as co amplitude of object, but as to analogy of the mode of communication. As Adam communicates sin to all his posterity and death through sin, so Christ bestows righteousness upon all his members and life through righteousness. So, Romans 5:18-19 is to be explained where a comparison is made between Adam and Christ, not as to extent, but as to similarity of operation. Thus, the world is taken for the whole of the elect and believers (2 Corinthians 5:19). In this sense, Augustine places two words in the idea of the world. "The whole world," he says, "is the church, and the whole world hates the church: the *world* (the lost) therefore hates the world (the church), the enemy the reconciled, the damned the saved," ("Tractate 87" On the Gospel of John [NPNFI, 7:355; PL 35.1853]; cf. also Prosper *The Call of the Nations* 1.3 [ACW 14:28]).

Judas who is the Son of Perdition.[26] But by not granting these instances, the scope of those for whom God, "so loves," is already limited. The scholarly puritan John Owen says, "First...Now, this love we say to be that, greater than which there is none. Secondly, by the "world," we understand the elect of God only, though not considered in this place as such, but under such a notion as, being true of them, serves for the farther exaltation of God's love towards them, which is the end here designed; and this is, as they are poor, miserable, lost creatures in the world, of the world, scattered abroad in all places of the world, not tied to Jews or Greeks, but dispersed in any nation, kindred, and language under heaven. The difference in the interpretation of this place is about the cause of sending Christ; called here love. Then about the object of this love; called here the world. Then, concerning the intention of God in sending his Son; said to be that believers might be saved."[27] As Owen again states, "It is the special love of God to his elect, as we affirm, and so, consequently, not any such thing as our adversaries

---

[26] "While I was with them in the world, I kept them in thy name: those that thou gavest me I have kept, and none of them is lost, but the son of perdition; that the scripture might be fulfilled," (John 17:12).

[27] Owen, John, *Works*, Vol. 10, 319ff (see his whole discourse). Quote cited from page 321.

supposed to be intended by it, namely, a velleity or natural inclination to the good of all."[28]

Francis Turretin, the Italian reformer, explains what the word "world" refers to. I quote him in brief here and in length in the footnote,

> "It is true of the elect alone that they are actually reconciled to God and that their sins will not be imputed unto them. Why then should "the world" not be taken universally for individuals, but indefinitely for anyone (Jews as well as Gentiles, without distinction of nation, language and condition) that he may be said to have loved the human race inasmuch as he was unwilling to destroy it entirely, but decreed to save some certain person out of it; not only from one people as before, but from all indiscriminately although the effects of that love should not be extended to each individual, but only to some certain ones (*viz.*, those chosen out of the world)! And nothing is more frequent in common conversation than to attribute to a community something with respect to some certain individual, not to all."[29]

---

[28] Ibid., 323.
[29] Turretin says, "The word "world" does not prove this love to be universal. Although it may be taken in common and indefinitely for the human race (as our Calvin, the Belgic commentators and others

interpret it), it does not follow that this love is to be referred to each and every one, but only that a peculiar privilege was bestowed upon the human race with respect to some particular part so that the entire species should not wholly perish. Indeed, this is in opposition: (1) to the family of angels to whom, in like sin, he did not grant like grace. Hence, he is called indeed philanthropist (philanthropos), but not philangelist (philangelos). If a prince of two rebellious states would utterly destroy the one sparing nobody, but so far spare the other as to rescue some certain ones from the common punishment destined to the others, he would be said to have entirely loved the one above the other although he might not have loved all the members of the latter equally because the good of the part resounds to the whole, and the denomination is made from the better. (2) It is in opposition to the economy of the Old Testament where salvation was given not to the world but to the Jewish nation alone to intimate that it was not sent for the Jews only, but also for the Gentiles indiscriminately. design of Christ to take away from Nicodemus the empty boastings in which the Jews were accustomed to indulge (and with which he also undoubtedly was fascinated), as if the Messiah had been promised and sent to his nation alone, and the other nations were either to be brought into subjection to them or to be cut off. In order, therefore, to meet the opinion of that nation (itself implanted and ready now to unfold the mystery of the calling of the Gentiles), he said that God loved the world, not only one nation or people. In this sense, he is called by the Samaritans "the Saviour of the "world" (John 4:42), *i.e.*, not only of the Jews (as under the Old Testament when salvation was only of the Jews, as Christ testifies, John 4:22), but also of the Gentiles. Thus, the worship of God would no longer be restricted as before to the temple of Jerusalem, but the true worshippers might everywhere worship in Spirit and in truth. Nor otherwise is Christ called by John the Baptist "the lamb of God which taketh away the sin of the world" (John 1:29), and by the evangelist "the propitiation not for our sins only" (i.e., the Jews) "but also for the sins of the whole world" (1 John 2:2), *i.e.* of the other nations. Thus, he would accomplish a common good to the whole church and designate those who at the same time were about to believe and who were scattered over various regions of the world (as Calvin explains it). Nor is it a new and unusual thing for "the world" to be taken not always in its whole latitude, but to be restricted to some certain ones out of the world: as when it is put for the Gentiles in opposition to the Jews, "if the fall of them be the riches of the world" (Romans 11:12); for the world of the wicked, of which Christ says, "I

Part 5: John 3:16

In dealing fairly with John, to understand 3:16, we must look through his Gospel and letters on the use of the word, "world."[30] Twenty-six times he uses the word to refer to the earth.[31] Three times he uses the word to refer to Jews and Gentiles specifically.[32] Twelve times he uses the word to refer to believers and unbelievers in the world, or all humanity.[33] Three times he uses the

---

pray not for the world" (John 17:9) and "the whole world lieth in wickedness" (1 John 5:19); for the world of believers when Christ says, "I will give my flesh for the life of the world" (John 6:51), not indeed of the world of the reprobate (who remain always in death), but of the elect (who are made alive through Christ); and "God was in Christ reconciling the world unto himself, not imputing their trespasses unto them" (2 Corinthians 5:19). It is true of the elect alone that they are actually reconciled to God and that their sins will not be imputed unto them. Why then should "the world" not be taken universally for individuals, but indefinitely for anyone (Jews as well as Gentiles, without distinction of nation, language and condition) that he may be said to have loved the human race inasmuch as he was unwilling to destroy it entirely, but decreed to save some certain person out of it; not only from one people as before, but from all indiscriminately although the effects of that love should not be extended to each." *Institutes*, Volume 1, 405-407.

[30] Each instance in the writings of John for the word "world" are as follows: John 1:9, 1:10, 1:29, 3:16, 3:17, 3:19, 4:42, 6:14, 6:33, 6:51, 7:4, 7:7, 8:12, 8:23, 8:26, 9:5, 9:32, 9:39, 10:36, 11:9, 11:27, 12:19, 12:25, 12:31, 12:46, 12:47, 13:1, 14:17, 14:19, 14:22, 14:27, 14:30, 14:31, 15:18, 15:19, 16:8, 16:11, 16:20, 16:21, 16:28, 16:33, 17:5, 17:6, 17:9, 17:11, 17:12, 17:13, 17:14, 17:15, 17:16, 17:18, 17:21, 17:23, 17:24, 17:25, 18:20, 18:36, 18:37, 21:25, 1 John 2:2, 2:15, 2:16, 2:17, 3:1, 3:13, 4:1, 4:3, 4:4, 4:5, 4:9, 4:14, 4:17, 5:4, 5:5, 5:19, 2 John 1:7, Revelation 3:10, 11:15, 12:9, 13:3, 13:8, 16:14, 17:8.

[31] The earth: John 13:1; 6:14; 9:5a; 9:32; 9:39; 10:36; 11:27; 16:21; 16:28; 17:5; 17:11a; 17:12; 17:23; 17:24; 18:36; 18:37; 21:25; 1John 4:1; 4:9; 2 John 1:7; Revelation 11:15; 13:8; 17:8.

[32] Jews and Gentiles: John 4:39; 18:20; Revelation 16:14.

[33] John 1:9-10; 3:17; 3:19; 7:4; 8:26; 9:5b; 12:19; 12:25; 14:30; 14:19; 16:11; Revelation 3:10.

word to refer to the world system in particular.[34] Thirty-one times he uses the word to refer to the wicked, without including believers, which is his most common use.[35] And finally, he uses the word for the world of the *elect* eleven times.[36] Seeing the varied usage of the word, the context and thought of each passage is critical, or the meaning of the word would enter into absurdity. For instance, if we were to use the same logic that contemporary Christians today[37] use in their use of the word "world" in John 3:16 as "everyone for all time", what dictates that we cannot use that same word in 1 John 5:19, "We know that we are of God, and the whole world lies under the sway of the wicked one." This would make absolutely no sense if we blanketed the word world to everyone for all time as those deceived for all time. Or what of Revelation 12:9, "So the great dragon was cast out, that serpent of old, called the Devil and Satan, who deceives the whole world; he was cast to the earth, and his angels were cast out with him." Is this the

---

[34] John 12:31; 1 John 5:19; 4:3-4.
[35] John 5:24; 7:7; 8:23; 12:31; 13:1; 14:17; 14:22; 14:31; 15:18-19; 16:8; 16:20; 17:6; 17:9; 17:11b; 17:15-16; 17:17; 17:21; 17:23; 17:25; 1 John 2:15-17; 3:1; 3:13; 4:5; 4:17; 5:4-5; Revelation 12:9; 13:3.
[36] John 1:29; 3:16; 3:17c; 6:33; 12:46-47; 6:51; 8:12; 11:9; 1 John 2:2; 4:14.
[37] *The Five Arminian Articles of the Remonstrance*, Article 2, "That agreeably thereto, Jesus Christ, the Savior of the world, died for all men and for every man, so that he has obtained for them all, by his death on the cross, redemption and the forgiveness of sins; yet that no one actually enjoys this forgiveness of sins except the believer according to the word of the Gospel of John 3:16..."

same all of humanity as they would purport in John 3:16? Is everyone deceived, including *you*, reader? Why do they read it into John 3:16 without considering the context of the "so" and the "gave", including the previous verse and the latter verse?

Arthur W. Pink also helps us further consider the word "world" in its context. He says,

> "But the objector comes back to John 3:16 and says, "World means world". True, but we have shown that "the world" does not mean the whole human family. The fact is that "the world" is used in a general way. When the brethren of Christ said, "Shew Thyself to the world" (John 7:4), did they mean "shew Thyself to all mankind?" When the Pharisees said, "Behold, the world is gone after Him" (John 12:19), did they mean that "all the human family" were flocking after Him? When the apostle wrote, "Your faith is spoken of throughout the whole world" (Romans 1:8), did he mean that the faith of the saints at Rome was the subject of conversation by every man, woman, and child on the earth? When Revelation 13:3 informs us that "all the world wondered after the beast," are we to understand that there will be no exceptions? What of the godly Jewish remnant, who will be slain

John 3:16

(Revelation 20:4) rather than submit? These, and other passages which might be quoted, show that the term "the world" often has a relative rather than an absolute force."[38]

I do believe that the word is relative depending on the context. In almost every instance it is used in the Bible it is *relative*. Seldom does it mean "the entire sphere called earth which includes people from all of time." It almost always has connotations to specific groups of people. Pink goes on to say, in 2 Corinthians 5:19 we read, "To wit that God was in Christ, reconciling the world unto Himself." What is meant by this is clearly defined in the words immediately following "not imputing their trespasses unto them." Here again, "the world" cannot mean "the world of the ungodly" for their trespasses are "imputed" to them, as the judgment of the Great White Throne will yet show. But 2 Corinthians 5:19 plainly teaches there is a "world" which are "reconciled", reconciled unto God, because their trespasses are not reckoned to their account, having been borne by their Substitute. Who then are they? Only one answer is fairly possible-the world of God's people! In like manner, the "world" in John 3:16 must, in the final analysis refer to *the world of God's people*. "Must," we

---

[38] See also Pink's further treatment of John 3:16 in *The Sovereignty of God*, (Grand Rapids: Baker Book House, 1999), 253.

say, for there is no other alternative solution. It cannot mean the whole human race, for one half of the race was already in hell when Christ came to earth. It is unfair to insist that it means every human being now living, for every other passage in the New Testament where God's love is mentioned limits it to his own people; take time to search this out and see for yourself! The objects of God's love in John 3:16 are precisely the same as the objects of Christ's love in John 13:1: "Now before the Feast of the Passover, when Jesus knew that His time was come, that He should depart out of this world unto the Father, having loved His own which were in the world, He loved them unto the end." I admit that my interpretation of John 3:16 is no innovative one invented on my own, but one almost uniformly given by the Reformers and Puritans, and many others since them.[39]

The Westminster Assembly also had some contentions concerning the idea of the word "world" due to the theological positions of the Amyraldians in their meetings (such as John Davenant). Rutherford, Seaman, and Gillespie contended for the word "world" as meaning "the elect" and presented the idea to the Assembly, and the Assembly accepted their proposition after presenting their study. God loves the "world" is God loving the "elect". This was noted in detail in their

---

[39] Consider reading Pink's, The Sovereignty of God, pages 200-203.

Minutes.[40] The consensus of the Assembly was to abandon the Amyraldian notion that God loves all men

---

[40] Gillespie, "In answer to the two arguments, one from John 3:16. The brother [a Mr. John Goodwin] takes for granted that by the world is meant the whole world. It is a point much controverted. Our divines do deny that the word world must in some places be taken in another sense...For that of philanthropy it makes much against it...I cannot understand how there can be such a universal love of God to mankind as is maintained. Those that will say it must needs deny the absolute reprobation; then alone to those whom God hath absolutely reprobated both from salvation and the means of salvation...For the next argument from Mark 16...He conceives the ground of this universal offer is the institution of Christ in dying...For that of the truth...There is a truth in it: the connection of those two extremes must ever hold true faith and salvation. But what is that to a reprobate? Here is the mistake. The *voluntas decreti* and *mandati* are not distinguished...A man is bound to believe that he ought to believe, and that by faith he shall be saved. It is his duty. The command does not hold out God's intentions; otherwise God's command to Abraham concerning sacrificing of his son...Said I cannot say so to a devil...True; but reason is, that it is the revealed will of God that devils are absolutely excluded, but not so any man known to me." Samuel Rutherford stated, "For the two scriptures alleged yesterday desire when I give a reason of the denial of a proposition...For that of John 3:16, three grounds of an argument taken from this place: 1. From the word loved; a general love to elect and reprobate. 2. From the word world, generally taken, because distributive afterwards. 3. Grounded upon God's intention upon condition of faith. For the first, Christ speaks of a particular special love...This all one with those places...This love is parallel, with that expressed in those three places...The love of one giving his life for his friends...the love that moved Him to send His only-begotten Son...If the love in John 3 be the same with those, as in those places is meant the special particular love of God commensurable with election...not one scripture in all the New Testament where it can be expounded for the general...2. The love in John 3 is restricted to the Church; Ephesians 5:25, restricted to a Church...so Galatians 2:20, loved me; the apostle who lives the life of God by faith...Romans 5:8, the sinners and ungodly are set down to be the justified by faith. Such a love as moved the husband Christ to give His life for His spouse, such as moved...such as God commends, for

generally[41] (following an Arminian scheme) and moved forward with the meaning of John 3:16 as particular for the elect only. The words, "He gave his only begotten Son" rest on the idea presented-the giving act of the Father.[42] The word gave (3rd person aorist active indicative of *didowmi*), is crucial to understanding God's intention in the passage. The Greek construction puts some stress on the actuality of the gift: it is not "God loved so as to give", but, "God loved *so that* he gave." His love is not a vaguely sentimental feeling, but a

---

the highest love is a restricted special love…3. It is an actual saving love, and therefore not a general love." *The Minutes of the Sessions of the Assembly of Divines*, (Edmunton: SWRB, n.d., 19**), 155.

[41] The Amyraldian concept derives from the order of decrees and the way the Amyraldian would think about how and when God would love men. They believed that God loved all men prior to the fall and then particularly after the fall. There is a great error created in that the decree to love does not come to pass. God's first decree (that he loved all men savingly) is thwarted by His second decree as a result of the fall. But even in this notion, the Amyraldian is inconsistent – for why would John 3:16, considered relevant after the fall, be speaking of God's love for all men before the fall? I believe the Amyraldian concept utterly fails on its own.

[42] Bunyan stresses the idea of the richness of God's love in His giving us His Son. John Bunyan, "Saved by Grace," in Master Christian Library, vol. 5 [CD-ROM] (Albany, Oregon: AGES Software, 1996), 23. He says, "The Father's grace ordaineth, and giveth the Son to undertake for us, our redemption. The Father sent the Son to be the Savior of the world: "In whom we have redemption through his blood, the forgiveness of sins, according to the riches of his grace; that in the ages to come he might shew the exceeding riches of his grace in his kindness to usward through Christ Jesus," 1 John 4:14; Ephesians 1:7, 2:7; John 3:16, 6:32, 33, 12:47."

love that costs. God gave what was most dear to him.[43] This is the love which is stated in Romans 8:31-32, "What then shall we say to these things? If God is for us, who can be against us? He who did not spare his own Son, but delivered him up for us all, how shall he not with Him also freely give us all things?" It is also that of 1 John 4:9-10, "In this the love of God was manifested toward us, that God has sent his only begotten Son into the world, that we might live through Him. In this is love, not that we loved God, but that He loved us and sent His Son to be the propitiation for our sins." Propitiation, God's love, and his giving are *all* intrinsically linked together here and paralleled in John 3:16. Keep in mind that the Apostle John wrote 3:16 and 1 John 4:9-10. It is clear that his (the Spirit's) intention is to echo Christ's teaching to Nicodemus. What does it mean to "give" the Son?[44] It is nothing less than the entirety of the oblation of Christ in his incarnation, work, death, resurrection, and intercession for the believer. In speaking of the giving, it points to the design

---

[43] Morris, Leon, *New International Commentary on the New Testament*, John (Grand Rapids: Wm. B. Eerdman's Publishing Co., 1989), 229-230.

[44] Owen, John, "Catechism: Of the Incarnation of Christ," in Master Christian Library, 43. Q. 4. What is the oblation of Christ? A. The offering up of himself, Isaiah 53:10, 12; John 3:16, upon the altar of the cross, 11:51, 17:19; Hebrews 9:13-14, an holy propitiatory sacrifice for the sins of all the elect throughout the world; as also, the presentation of Hebrews 9:24, himself for *us* in heaven, sprinkled with the blood of the covenant."

and intention of God. The puritan John Flavel states, "You have heard of the gracious purpose and design of God, to recover poor sinners to himself by Jesus Christ, and how this design of love was laid and contrived in the covenant of redemption, whereof we last spake. Now, according to the terms of that covenant, you shall hear from this scripture, how that design was by one degree advanced towards its accomplishment, in God's actual giving or parting with his own Son for us: 'God so loved the world, that he gave,' etc. The whole precedent context is spent in discovering the nature and necessity of regeneration, and the necessity thereof is in this text urged and inferred from the peculiar respect and eye God had upon believers, in giving Christ for them; they only reaping all the special and saving benefits and advantages of that gift: "God so loved the world, that he gave his only begotten Son, that whosoever believeth in him should not perish."[45]

Compare John 3:16 with John 6:33. If people believe world is *all men for all time*, if they are consistent in their hermeneutic, they should see the same result of the word *world* in 6:33. "For the bread of God is he which cometh down from heaven, and *giveth life unto the world*." If this is true, and we were to use the same

---

[45] Flavel, John, "Sermon: Opens the Admirable love of God in Giving His Own Son for Us," *The Works of John Flavel*, vol. 1 (Carlisle: Banner of
Truth Trust, 1968).

interpretive tools that some have used on John 3:16, then, as Jesus gives life to the world, they all, by necessity, *must* have life and are alive. But we know the "world is condemned already" if they remain in unbelief, according to 3:18. How could we interpret John 6:33 to mean "all men for all time?" We cannot, just as we cannot say he loved, "all men for all time," in John 3:16. Who are these which are given life? We know the whole world is not given life or *they would be alive*. If they eat of the bread of life, then they have life. Jesus is not saying that he is the bread of life which gives life to every man for all time so all men are regenerated. He is saying that all men, Jews and Gentiles, may eat of him. Not *every* individual man, but *all kinds* of men, which would have been completely foreign to the twisted and warped fallen ears of Nicodemus. As a matter of fact, in John 6:41 the Jews murmured at his teaching, saying that Jesus could not have "come down from heaven" since he is "Joseph's son." But Jesus then remarks to them in 6:43-44 with these words, "Murmur not among yourselves. No man can come to me, except the Father which hath sent me draw him: and I will raise him up at the last day." This shows the *intention* of God towards the Jews, and towards the world. He raises up only those that the Father gives him. The Father, if he were *savingly* interested in all men, would *have given* all men to Christ. But God is not interested in all men in this way, but only some men—those Jesus will raise up at the last day. These are the ones for whom the Son of Man is lifted up in public view, and these are the ones drawn by cords of love to the Father.

    The "giving" of Christ is of intense theological importance. Even the Greek construction given to these words shows us the rarity and exclamational intent of John as the writer, and Jesus as the Son of Man. The phrase, "that he gave" is the usual classical construction of the grammar with "hoste" and the indicative (first aorist active) which entail a practical result; that God did do such a thing as give his Son, truly. The only other example of this in the New Testament is in Galatians 2:13 where Paul is shocked that even Barnabas was "carried away" (given to them) with the hypocrisy of the Jews which seemed unthinkable.[46] Why did God do all this giving? John Owen states, "The whole Scripture constantly assigneth this sole end of that effect of divine goodness and wisdom; yea, asserts it as the only foundation of the Gospel, John 3:16."[47] God gave because of his goodness to the elect and his goodness is seen in the covenant of the Gospel itself, not specifically to all men in general. The divine goodness and wisdom of God has given Christ as a sacrifice, and offering to "whosoever believes." Those "ho pisteuow," *the*

---

[46] Robertson, *Word Pictures*, 50.
[47] Owen, *Christologia*, 242.

believing ones, partake of what God gave in his love, "his only begotten Son." To "believe" is immediately linked to Jesus' instruction in verse 3, those who are "born again" and who "spiritually perceive" the things of the Kingdom. Those believing are those sovereignly regenerated by the Spirit who gives birth to spirit. The construction here is considered a "purpose clause"[48] in the Greek. It is impossible to break the line of Christ's thought and ascribe the special and purposeful love of God which gives his only begotten Son to the entirety of mankind without distinction, where Jesus has, in verse 3 and following, *already* made the distinction.[49]

Most Christians and even some well-respected theologians assign John 3:16 to all men generally. But this would be to deviate from the context. John Owen rightly states, "Nor is there any mention of any special love or grace of God unto sinners, but with respect unto the satisfaction of Christ[50] as the means of the

---

[48] A purpose clause designates a construction that states the purpose involved in some other action; for example, "John came in order to help him." Graham S. Ogden and Lynell Zogbo, *A Handbook on Ecclesiastes*, (New York: United Bible Societies, 1998), 460.

[49] This distinction is already present in the idea of "whoever believes."

[50] Owen, *Christologia*, 242. Q. 2. Died he for no other? A. None, in respect of his Acts 20:28; Matthew 20:28, 26:28; Father's eternal purpose, and Hebrews 9:28; John 11:51, 52; his own intention of removing Isaiah 53:12; John 3:16, wrath from them, and 10:11-13,15; Ephesians 5:25; Romans procuring grace and glory for 8:32, 34; Galatians 3:13; them. John 6:37, 39; Romans 4:25; 2 Corinthians 5:19, 20.

communication of all its effects unto them."[51] John Gerstner states, "John 3:16 says more clearly than probably any verse in Scripture that the atonement was made for believers only. God so loved the world He gave His Son that believers should have eternal life."[52] Even John Newton states that God in John 3:16 "opened the Kingdom of God to all *believers.*"[53] The Kingdom of God is open to *every believer*, but that is a limited number; and they are those who are birthed from above, beget by the Spirit, and whom God regenerates and endows with

---

[51] See Owen's "The Doctrine of Justification," in Master Christian Library, vol. 5, 92. See John 3:16; Romans 3:23-25; 8:30-33; 2 Corinthians 5:19-21; Ephesians 1:7; *etc.*

[52] Gerstner, John, *Wrongly Dividing the Word of Truth*, (Morgan, PA: Soli Deo Gloria, 1991) 139-140, "We first consider the very common misunderstanding of John 3:16. It is supposed to teach that God so loved everyone in the world that He gave His only Son to provide them an opportunity to be saved by faith. What is wrong with this interpretation? First, such a "love" on God's part, so far from being love, would be the refinement of cruelty. As we have already seen, offering a gift of life to a spiritual corpse, a brilliant sunset to a blind man, and a reward to a legless cripple if only he will come and get it, are horrible mockeries. The reason the dispensationalists do not see this is because, though they profess to believe in total depravity, they are in fact Arminian. Second, the verse clearly states for whom this love gift was given. "He gave His only begotten Son, that whoever believes in Him should not perish." John 3:16 says more clearly than probably any verse in Scripture that the atonement was made for believers only. God so loved the world He gave His Son that believers should have eternal life. Third, since even Arminians admit that believers are elect, even Arminians should see that John 3:16 has in plainest possible language said that God gave His only Son that the elect (*whoever* believes) "should not perish have everlasting life."

[53] John Newton, *The Works of John Newton*, Volume 2, (Carlisle: Banner of Truth Trust, 1988), 285-286.

the ability to exercise faith in the Redeemer. It is the intention of God towards, "whosoever believes," that determines the, "world," of the verse, and the direction of his saving goodness and his love. Think about how this would have come across to Nicodemus. The Jews were God's chosen people. Salvation is *for the Jews*, God's elect nation. To say that "whoever believes" can be saved, and that God loved the "world," as in all kinds and types of people, would be to disrupt, again, Nicodemus in his understanding of what he has always believed as a Jew. The Son of Man has a right over all peoples, tribes and nations, and has dominion over the world. He is able, by his Spirit to choose elect individuals from all over the world. Yes, Nicodemus, even Gentiles!

The objection is often stated as such, "God's love is infinite, and it cannot be limited to only a few." God's saving love is not as indiscriminate as his providence is over the whole earth. The Scottish Puritan Samuel Rutherford answers well for us if the former is true; "this should conclude, that there be an infinite number of men and angels to whom God's salvation is betrothed in affection; but his love is infinite in its act, not in its object; the way of carrying on His love is infinite."[54] But the idea continues into the concept that because God is love, then God must, out of necessity to his nature, love.

---

[54] Samuel Rutherford, Trial and Triumph of Faith (London: Pilgrim Book House, 1645), (reprinted in Carmichael, CA, 1991), 16.

This love then encompasses all of creation in one form or another. But the passage simply *does not teach this*. This is not Jesus' point to the Pharisee. There must be a distinction between love *ad infra* and *ad extra; i.e.* within the nature of the Trinity, there is a pure love communicated to each of the persons of the Trinity. The Father loves the Son and the Son loves the Father and this love is communicated between them through the working of the Spirit of love. This love is the inner Trinitarian love which is *ad infra*, a love *without* restriction. God, communicating love in this way, holds a pure and unrestricted love. Yet, there is also a pouring out of his love in and through Christ, which is restricted to those elected in Christ, and joined in union to him.[55] This pouring out of redemptive love on his creatures is *ad extra*, outside himself in the Beloved.[56] As finite creatures it would be impossible to receive the saving love of God in any other form except through the mediation of Christ since the love which God pours out is *infinite. Finitum non capax infinitum*[57] is the general rule which must always be attended to when understanding the communication of God's attributes

---

[55] For a full discussion of this union, see John Brinsley's masterful work, *The Christian's Union, Communion and Conformity to Jesus Christ In His Death and Resurrection*, published by Puritan Publications.
[56] Ephesians 1:6 speaks about the elect's acceptance, *"in the Beloved."*
[57] The finite cannot contain the infinite.

to his people. We cannot contain the love which God shares *ad infra*. We obtain and enjoy, through God's gift of being born from above, that which is in Christ *ad extra*.[58]

John Owen speaks about the love of God in this manner when he states, "He is love eternally and necessarily in this love of the Son; all other workings of love are but acts of His will, whereby somewhat of it is outwardly expressed."[59] Here Owen says that God necessarily loves in Christ but those acts of love externally upon men are those which he wills as a "love of the creature" or "love of men" but not a salvific love. God, then, will savingly love men in wisdom. He uses his goodness and love wisely in specific acts of his will upon his creation. Owen continues to explain that God's love is experienced by us in the, "person of Christ...the first recipient subject of all that divine love which extends itself unto the church. It is all, the whole of it, in the first place fixed upon him, and by and through him is communicated unto the church."[60] God does not exercise his saving love unwisely, or irrespective of Christ. Turretin states this same thought,

---

[58] And in our finite nature, we only experience and can discern a limited amount of what this means.
[59] Owen, *Works*, Volume 1, 144.
[60] Ibid., 146. See also John 3:35; John 5:20; Matthew 3:17; Matthew 17:5.

> "Hence although love is considered affectively and on the part of the internal act is equal in God (because it does not admit of increase or diminution), yet regarded effectively (or in the part which He wills to anyone) it is unequal because some effects of love are greater than others."

John Calvin states,

> "Since our hearts cannot, in God's mercy, either seize upon life ardently enough or accept it with the gratefulness we owe, unless our minds are first struck and overwhelmed by fear of God's wrath and by dread of eternal death, we are taught by Scripture to perceive that apart from Christ, God is, so to speak, hostile to us, and his hand is armed for our destruction; to embrace his benevolence and fatherly love in Christ alone."[61]

Here Calvin also says that this kind of benevolence is found *in Christ alone*. He says, "until Christ succours us by his death, the unrighteousness that deserves God's indignation remains in us, and is accursed and condemned before Him."[62] God loves *himself in us*. God

---
[61] Calvin, Institutes, vol. 1, 505. (2.16.3)
[62] Ibid., 506. (*Institutes*, 2.16.3)

loves *Christ in us*. He does not love the fallen wickedness, the wicked intents and thoughts of our hearts. He loves Christ, and when we are *in Christ,* he loves us *ad extra*.⁶³

It is also important to make note of the word "whosoever" in the Greek. The text is often rendered, "that whosoever believes shall have everlasting life." Appeal is made to the "whosoever" and not commonly to "whosoever believes." The Gospel is certainly a "whosoever believes" Gospel, but there is a more important note to make on this word than stressing the obvious fact that the "whosoever" is linked with "belief." John 3:16 (as the Greek was fully quoted previously) part of the verse is ἵνα πᾶς **ὁ πιστεύων** εἰς αὐτὸν μὴ ἀπόληται, "whosoever believes" idea, the word in bold type is a verb which is a participle. It is the present active nominative masculine singular verb which determines our English rendering, "whosoever believes". The problem here is the word, "whosoever". There is no word

---

⁶³ See also Augustine on this in *Nicene and Post Nicene Fathers*, Volume 7, 411. Here Augustine treats the love of God in Christ and then in us as he expounds John 17. This can be found in <u>Tractate 110</u>. Augustine states, "For He could not but love the members of His Son seeing that He loveth the Son Himself; nor is there any reason for loving His members, save that He loveth Himself." Augustine will show how God loves the Son from all eternity as the Son, then Christ as Christ, and then us in Him as Christ is in us. God loves in us that which is himself. See my work, *Augustine's Calvinism* for a full treatment of his ideas surrounding the *giving* of Christ in salvation.

"whosoever" in the Greek text. Literally the section reads "the believing ones into him," as the phrase is written. God so loved the world that the ones who believed in Christ may not perish but have everlasting life. As hard as this is to accept for Nicodemus, it is equally hard for most of Christendom today to accept what Jesus is saying. Oftentimes Christians stress the word, "whosoever," where the word does not even exist in the original. The Gospel as it pertains to eternal life, here, is directed to those *who believe*, and to no others. Even if we were to take liberty in rendering the English as, "whosoever believes", it still ends up meaning the same thing: that those believing—whosoever they may be— are the ones actually saved.[64] Instead, Christians try and turn this around to say that anyone *can* believe, which is opposite to the entire discourse of John 3. John 3:16 is not directed towards the entirety of mankind

---

[64] R.K. McGregor Wright states, "The passage states that as a result of his loving the world, God gave his Son, which is usually understood to be a reference to the incarnation and atonement. Then the Greek says "in order that every one believing in him may not perish." There is no word for "whosoever" in the original. On the contrary, far from God's giving his Son to provide a generalized atonement for everyone who exists, the verse states that he gave his Son for the express purpose of saving a special group. Since this group excludes all unbelievers and is less than all existing human beings, John 3:16 states explicitly that the purpose of God in sending his Son to die was limited to atoning for believers only, that they "should not perish, but have everlasting life." This is what Calvinists call a limited atonement, in answer to the general or universal atonement taught by the Arminian, Catholic and Lutheran systems." Wright, *No Place for Sovereignty*, 159.

with no exceptions. Christians sometimes refuse this for an interpretation which views this as a *general* saving love. However, those suffering in hell, or who will suffer in hell, are not the recipients of the cross of Christ and the benefits of the redeeming love of God towards the elect, but would be considered part of the whole world. If these Christians are merely stating that God has an eye, now, towards all nations instead of simply to Israel, then such an interpretation would still warrant the specific aspect that I am exegetically proving by the text. God's love in John 3:16 is the highest form of love, as the Greek shows us, and that love cannot be towards the whole world *indiscriminately* with a lesser love to the elect. Nor can this love be both for the whole world *and* the elect, for then we would wonder why the whole world is not saved because when God gives Christ to be a sacrifice and saves people, *Christ is doing the saving*, not the people. Neither its context, nor its use of the Greek, allows its use to aid in propagating a general love for all men; nor is this the point of the passage. This love cannot be extended to all without distinction, but to all kinds (both Jew and Gentile) from all ages with the distinct and particular love of God in Christ to his elect in those masses.[65] So, Jesus is teaching Nicodemus, a

---

[65] Here is a small list of writers who believe John 3:16 is to the elect world: Augustine, John Calvin, Francis Turretin, Martin Bucer, John Flavel, Augustus Toplady, Jerome Zanchius, Robert Haldane, John Knox, Martin Luther, Christopher Love, Jonathan Edwards,

Jewish ruler, that his narrow Pharisaical interpretation of God's love is wrong.

The saving love of God in Christ does not simply fall upon the Jew, but all kinds of men, the Gentiles included.

Jesus is not saying that God's love is a general saving love for all men indiscriminately, but it reaches to all nations indiscriminately under the new covenant. However, even though sound Christians rest on this interpretation, they must at the very least agree with me that the elect of Christ, are those which this saving love shall be ultimately applied. This does not destroy the message of John 3:16, but rather enforces it. Jesus had been teaching Nicodemus in John 3:1-10 that the Spirit of God moves as the wind blows and regenerates whom he will. This is God's eternal decree realized in the lives of men. In verse 16, he stresses the work of God on the world through the Son of Man. God reaches out into the entire world to gather his elect. His elect, do not only reside in the physical covenant community of Israel any longer, but through the farthest reaches of the whole

---

John Owen, Lorraine Boettner, John Newton, John Bunyan, William Whittaker, Thomas Doolittle, Samuel Annesley, Thomas Vincent, The Westminster Divines, John Gerstner, R.C. Sproul, and R. K. McGregor Wright. The following are those who do not believe John 3:16 as special love to the elect, but a general love to all men for all time: Matthew Henry, Charles Spurgeon, John Murray, Ezekiel Hopkins, J.C. Ryle, and R.L. Dabney.

John 3:16

world-all peoples, tribes and nations. This is something this Pharisee would have certainly rejected.

Study Questions for Part 5

1. What are some uses of the word "world" that could not mean what is intended *as all men for all time?*

2. Why is "so" so important in John 3:16?

3. What kind of love does God have for those of John 3:16?

4. How does God's love compare to other kinds of love God might have for mankind in general?

5. What is the Greek idea behind "whosoever believes?"

6. The believing ones are those who have eternal life. What is the essence of Jesus' teaching on eternal life?

7. God gave the Israelites sacrifices in the Old Testament for the people "inside the camp." Does the sacrifice on the Day of Atonement apply to the Philistines, Amorites, Jebusites, *etc.*? How does God in *giving* Christ fulfill God intention in Christ's sacrifice on the cross?

8. How does *God loving the world* coincide with God's just judgment on men currently in hell?

John 3:16

9. Can Esau be hated and loved by God at the same time and in the same sense? Why or why not?

10. Christ said, "It is finished," on the cross; what was he referring to?

11. Did Jesus make a way of salvation on the cross, or did he actually save people on the cross? And what are the implications of Christ being the only *Savior* if he saves *on the cross*, in completing and obtaining his work and merit for sinners?

Part 6:
John 3:17-21

"For God sent not his Son into the world to condemn the world; but that the world through him might be saved," (John 3:17).

The world sits in contrast to Nicodemus' theological errors. God is reaching across the globe to reign in his people. This is something Nicodemus should be engaging in with all his Pharisee brothers. But instead of reaching outwardly in missionary endeavors to fulfill God's promises to Abraham that he would be the father to many nations, the rulers of the Jews looked inwardly. They set up a system that created outward pomp and circumstance under the title of religion. Jesus corrected all this with Nicodemus in a few short, but powerful verses.

Connected to God's redemption of mankind in verse 16, verse 17 further explains the mission of the *lifted up Son of Man*. He is not coming to open the books and judge the world...right now. That will come later on. Instead, Christ explains that the nations are being given an opportunity to repent and be saved. All nations, Gentiles as well as Jews, are being given precious time to come to understand the truth of the Savior. He is not just the Savior of the Jews, but of the world.[1]

Jesus says, "He that believeth on him is not condemned: but he that believeth not is condemned already, because he hath not believed in the name of the only begotten Son of God," (John 3:18). Nicodemus should understand the meaning behind the power of the Son of Man who has come to earth. The Jews would have originally thought the Messiah was initially to come to judge Israel's physical enemies. But this is not the plan of the Redeemer. Judgment, though, is not necessarily suspended. The Son of Man instructs the Pharisee that those who believe on him are not condemned. There is no condemnation for "the believing ones." There will never be any judgmental eye towards final damnation to any of those who truly believe on the one and only Son of God. In contrast, group two has an eternal problem. We do not have to wait for judgment for those that do not believe. They stand *condemned already* who will not believe in the Son of God as the Redeemer of mankind. Nicodemus' Pharisaical rejection of inward belief for outward show is a demonstration of *practical atheism*

---

[1] There are theological implications of saying this in this particular way. Time, really *time to repent*, is somewhat of a misnomer in certain respects. Such is the case with the biblical concept of people or peoples filling up the measure of their sin, or gaining a certain amount of spiritual light only to be condemned by their misuse of it. But that is not an issue to deal with in this little work.

and the rejection of the Messiah. Such people stand condemned now, and they do not need to wait for the Son of Man to return on clouds of glory to open up books and judge them face to face (though Christ will do that anyway). They stand condemned for their unbelief. Judgment is already on them *in* their disbelief.

Jesus then returns to statements about the heart as a way of commenting on the ability or non-ability to believe on the Son of Man. "And this is the condemnation, that light is come into the world, and men loved darkness rather than light, because their deeds were evil," (John 3:19). The Son of Man, the light of the world, has come from heaven to teach men the truth of heavenly things, and the plan of a God who reaches across time and space to save sinners. But the judgment and verdict *is already in* because of the fall of Adam. Men love darkness instead of the light. Why? Their natures are evil, and evil natures give way to evil deeds. Men would much rather love their sin and the evil that they engage in against God, than for one moment consider what benefit the light may have on their life. And it may be, as with Nicodemus, that evil men may have heard the truth of the Son of Man, but still reject it. It is not, in Nicodemus' case, a lack of knowledge at this point, but rather a commentary on his heart – his deeds are evil. Again, what would Nicodemus be thinking here?

"For every one that doeth evil hateth the light, neither cometh to the light, lest his deeds should be reproved," (John 3:20). Jesus explains that evil deeds *come from* evil hearts. These are the hearts of stone that the Spirit must regenerate and make hearts of flesh. Evil people hate the light of the Gospel, the Gospel light that the Son of Man brings down from heaven having perfect communion with the Father. They hate this Gospel, and they hate the manner in which God expresses the Gospel because they are repelled by the light of his nature. There is a great worthiness in walking with God in the Spirit according to the example of Christ, to increase in holiness, by walking in the light. "...that you may walk worthy of the Lord, fully pleasing Him, being fruitful in every good work and increasing in the knowledge of God," (Col. 1:10). Walking in the Spirit is walking *in* the light, and it is a means of fellowship with God, and with the saints. "But if we walk in the light as He is in the light, we have fellowship with one another, and the blood of Jesus Christ His Son cleanses us from all sin," (1 John 1:7). Walking in the light means Christians have fellowship with God by the blood of Christ. If Christians say they love God, if they live to God, then they walk in the Spirit and walk with God, according to his commandments, and his word.

The wicked's evil hearts revolt against everything the light stands for because all of the thoughts of their heart are *only* evil continually, (Genesis 6:5). And if they would walk into the light, without the regenerating power of the Spirit of God, they would see the blackest darkness held within their hearts that which is infinitely overwhelming to their soul. Their conscience, so long as it is not terribly seared, presses them to consider their sin in light of the Law of God, but they suppress this. *They hate this light and cannot come into the light on their own. They run from the light as fast as they are |able, and they cover up their wickedness by attempting to replace the darkness of their heart with something else; in this case, Nicodemus used outward religion.*[2] You, reader, may use something else like sports, or hobbies, or family, or the like. In the end, men, kings, nobles, princes, peoples of all kinds will call for the mountains to fall on them, lest their deeds be exposed to the radiance of God's shekinah glory and the Son of Man that comes in the power of God's spoken word and perfect judgment (*cf.* Rev. 6:16ff).

---

[2] "Light" is the root word of 'enlightenment,' synonymous with knowledge, understanding, awareness and wisdom (*i.e.*, truth). It is also associated with "seeing," since one cannot see in the dark. Light is necessary for seeing, and the more light one has, the better they can see. It's not surprising, then, that Scripture refers to our all-seeing God as light, (1 John 1:5), the Father of lights, (James 1:17), dwelling in unapproachable light, (1 Tim. 6:16). Jesus refers to himself in the Gospels as the Light of the world, (John 8:12) and John in one of his letters to fellow believers encourages Christians to walk in the light as God is in the light, (1 John 1:7). There is no darkness in him at all (1 John 1:5), nothing in his being or outside of his being is hidden from his understanding.

Jesus ends this discourse with verse 21, which is an invitation of sorts, "But he that doeth truth cometh to the light, that his deeds may be made manifest, that they are wrought in God," (John 3:21). *Where the unbelievers rush into the domain of darkness, rejecting the light, those in contrast, who have been made believers by the Spirit's work, come into the light.* Why do they come into the light? They love the truth because they are made to love the truth.[3] Believers cannot do anything but to love the truth and hear the voice of the Shepherd, the Son of Man, calling them into the light. Truth doers are light bearers. Truth doers are those which hear the Shepherd calling and respond. Only sheep hear the voice of the Shepherd, where goats reject the call. Truth doers desire to have their deeds exposed because their sinful works are replaced with the work of the Son of Man lifted up. It is Christ's righteousness that clothes their dark, evil deeds, and they are washed away in God's love for them. They are now vessels that hold the work that God works in them and through them.[4]

What, then, did Nicodemus do? We do not read of his response. There is no happy ending to the narrative. There is introduction, dialogue, didactic teaching and then, *nothing*. But, what *should*

---

[3] cf. the passage of 1 John 1:6-9.
[4] "Being confident of this very thing, that he which hath begun a good work in you will perform it until the day of Jesus Christ," (Phil. 1:6).

Nicodemus do? He should come out of the darkness and into the light. He should do this by an active, real interest in the Son of Man lifted up. But he cannot do this until the Spirit changes his heart and gives him newness of life. He should, then, place himself under every means to attain that end. Speaking with Jesus here is a good start.

Later in the Gospel of John, we do find that Nicodemus speaks for the truth in John 7:50-51, where he says, "Nicodemus, who had gone to him before, and who was one of them, said to them, "Does our law judge a man without first giving him a hearing and learning what he does?" (John 7:50-51). This was a safe answer, but a true one, on account of the Pharisees' desire to overthrow the Son of Man who had come from heaven to usher in the true Kingdom of God. Then in John 19:39, we find Nicodemus participating in the removal of Jesus' body and the preparation to bury him, "Nicodemus also, who earlier had come to Jesus by night, came bringing a mixture of myrrh and aloes, about seventy-five pounds in weight." Could it be in the course of time that Nicodemus came to faith? We pray that it is so.

Study Questions for Part 6

1. What does it mean to be *condemned already?*

2. Why do men love darkness? Why do they not want to come into the light of the truth of the Gospel?

3. What is "light"? What is the relationship between *truth* and *light?*

4. What is God working *in* believers, and why do believers love coming into the light even though their sins will be exposed?

Part 7: Final Thoughts

Mr. Potato Head takes center stage in most contemporary and popular Christian theology books and churches. What do I mean by this? If you buy a Mr. Potato Head for your children (that famous toy in the toy store), you would see that it is packaged *blank*. It gives you, however, all the necessary parts, (lips, eyes, ears, *etc.*) to make your *very own* Mr. Potato Head just the way you would like it. It's a blank canvas, a blank potato, and you dress him up as you desire. In the neighboring cities surrounding God's Old Testament church, the people often infected the Israelites with their pagan gods and idols (Lev. 19:4; 2 Kings 17:12; 1 Chron. 16:26; 2 Chron. 24:18; Ezek. 44:10). They were made out of wood, stone, silver or gold, and created to represent some image that the one fashioning it made as a likeness – a fish, a bull, *etc.* Then after fashioning it, they bowed down to it to worship it.

Today, "Mr. Potato Head idolatry" is the new rage. People fashion their own ideas about God based on what they think God should be like. People desire a God who is only "love" without wrath, justice or holiness. They fashion a God who has a deep, earnest love with every individual who has ever lived, at the expense of his other attributes, because they think that God's *best* attribute is love. Love to what? *Love to me.* He is waiting in heaven, beckoning for man to make the first move. He does what he can in wooing them to come to him, but he is altogether powerless against the sovereignty of man's free will. This is not the God that Christ spoke to Nicodemus about; no, it is not the God of the Bible. Professing Christians love to retain thoughts of a "god" who says to humankind, "whosoever will..." This would infer that everyone, even Esau, Judas and Pharaoh, even those suffering in hell, have a chance to be saved, and every sinner has the power to "will" themselves towards that end, so that, then, the Holy Spirit can come and give them the new birth. Such an impotent "god" is idolatry, and has no place in the biblical thought of truly born-again Christians. It is not the Son of Man coming in the clouds of glory who has dominion over all people, languages, tribes and nations. John 3:16 is very clear, "For God loved the world so much, that he sent his one and only Son, that everyone who believes shall not perish but have life everlasting." There is no "whosoever," so to speak. Jesus taught Nicodemus that true sight is a product, first, of the Holy Spirit's work in giving birth to men by way of a new heart, so that men may be able to believe. He taught Nicodemus that, "everyone who believes on Christ goes to heaven." Nicodemus would have quickly thought back to the words of Christ just moments before to answer the question, "How do I believe?" Here the faithful exegete, along with the

Pharisee, retraces his steps to the first verses of chapter 3, John 3:1-10. He reminds himself of Christ's teaching, that the Spirit must *first* cause a man's heart to be transformed, to be born again, and then the spirit of a man comes willingly to God, seeing, spiritually, his need of a Savior. To place saving faith *before* regeneration (the tools to enact faith) is to disregard the plain meaning of the text here. And if we change the text to fit our theological stance, then we believe in a different "god" and a different way of salvation than Christ taught us. This new fabricated "god" is so powerless that he cannot even open a human heart! That "god" is weak, impotent and servile. It is *not* the God of the Bible, but of man's imaginations (and consider Genesis 6:5 on that note).

It is unfortunate that Christ, through his Word, is still saying the very same things to the church at large today, "you are teachers...and you do not understand such things?" Let us hear Christ's words and believe him at his word (the plain meaning of the passage once we understand what it is saying to us), listening to the voice of the Shepherd, remembering that we can only take his words to heart if the Spirit has blown on us and regenerated it in the first place.

For, God so loved his elect in Christ from every tribe, tongue and nation, that he sent the Son of Man, the only Son of his love, to come and teach us about the Father, about heaven, about his redemption, that everyone who is regenerated and believes the message of the Gospel, will not perish, or stand condemned in judgment, both now and to come, and instead, will have eternal life and communion with God in truth and light forever and ever. Amen.

Part 8: Your Spiritual Birth

We have seen what Christ says concerning the work of the Holy Spirit in making some men born from above, and the intention of God in his love to save his elect people from death and hell out of all nations, tribes and peoples. Redemption only occurs through the saving work of Jesus Christ, God's one and only Son, the Son of Man, who comes down from heaven to testify of the true communion men may again have with God the Father through him. Though we have been speaking both theologically and practically concerning John 3, there is an important need to bring this home to you, the reader.

Are *you* born from above? If you know you are not, then this little book may be genuinely confusing to you. If you think you are saved, but you are not actually converted, this book will be equally confusing, but in a different way. You are like Nicodemus who thought he had a good relationship with God, but didn't. If you are truly born from above, regenerated by the Holy Spirit, and have believed on Christ for your salvation based on the message of the Gospel, but have sat under poor teaching for one year, or many years in your church, then this little book might be a deep theological exercise that is causing you to stretch your mind to really ponder what John 3 is teaching you. If you are born again, born from above, have been changed by the Holy Spirit and have found the Bible as it was meant to be – a love letter sent to you from Christ, and you come regularly to the deep well of Christ's rich grace, this work may be a means to your further sanctification in holiness. Deeper thoughts of Christ are used by the Holy Spirit to deepen our walk with the Father (who desires that we are worshippers who know him intimately).[1]

Finally, if you are a Christian who is born again, and have heard all these same ideas before, having previously studied this passage, then count it a blessing that you have a mind that thinks the same way the historic Christian church has thought for two thousand years concerning these important verses. You sit in good company. And it is a blessing, then, to hear the narrative again, and be blessed by recalling the word of Christ as a sheep who hears his voice clearly.[2]

However, for all of those who are not born again, you are in a dire predicament. Christ will not commit himself to you until the Spirit of God changes your heart.[3] God is certainly willing to change sinners into saints, but it is not at the expense of his character in

---

[1] See John 4 and Romans 12:1-2.
[2] "My sheep hear my voice, and I know them, and they follow me," (John 10:27). "But if any man love God, the same is known of him," (1 Cor. 8:3).
[3] "But Jesus did not commit himself unto them, because he knew all men," (John 2:24).

holiness or justice. That means, until you place yourself under the means by which God ordinarily uses to change a sinner's stony heart to a heart of flesh, then you will remain in your sin. That means sitting under the preaching of the word, under a serious preacher. Those who remain in sin are liable to all the punishments of being in a state which makes them the enemies of God.[4] You may have enemies right now in the regular course of your life. They may dislike you for a number of reasons. They may call you names, embarrass you, despise you for one reason or another, even wish you harm. But human enemies are not like having God as your enemy, or being at war with God. God is much worse than a mere human, and is infinitely powerful. Imagining having God as your enemy? Can you conceive of it? He sees all you do, he is present with you at every conception of sin, and he has the power to judge you justly, and render a righteous punishment on you for all eternity.

Because you are born judicially under the sin of Adam and his fall,[5] God has reckoned your account, even at the day of your conception, as fallen, wicked, evil and against his character.[6] God requires that every person be

---

[4] "Do you not know that friendship with the world is enmity with God? Therefore whoever wishes to be a friend of the world makes himself an enemy of God," (James 4:4).
[5] "For as in Adam *all* die," (1 Cor. 15:22).
[6] "The wicked are estranged from the womb: they go astray as soon as they be born, speaking lies," (Psalm 58:3).

perfect in his sight.⁷ But being fallen in Adam necessarily makes you imperfect at the start. Then, throughout your life you sin, and those sins you commit aggravate your already fallen condition.⁸ God not only is forced to judge you on the actions of Adam's fall, but also your own actions which stem from that fall. Judgment, as we have seen from Christ's teaching to Nicodemus, is something, then, that you have on you right now remaining in a state of unbelief.⁹ Christ will not commit himself to you in the same way he did not commit himself to the sinful crowd who thought the goodness of religious acts were something to be outwardly seen. But as we also saw in Christ's teaching, there is hope.

Being born again, or being regenerated by the Holy Spirit (born from above) concerns three stages, 1) when the Lord plants new life in your dead heart, 2) when you as the new-born man believe the Gospel, 3) when your conversion transitions into sanctification (the process of being made more holy). The Holy Spirit may affect all this in the sinner's heart before, during or after the preaching of the word of God. But the preaching of the word is the primary vehicle that God

---

[7] "Be ye therefore perfect, even as your Father which is in heaven is perfect," (Matthew 5:48).
[8] "Verily I say unto thee, Thou shalt by no means come out thence, till thou hast paid the uttermost farthing," (Matt. 5:26).
[9] "But whoever does not believe is condemned already, because he has not believed in the name of the only Son of God," (John 3:18).

uses to change your stony heart to a heart that beats after him.[10]

Salvation depends on faith, and faith depends on the hearing of the word in most ordinary cases. That is God's regularly ordained means to affect salvation in an individual. "He who works in man both to will and to do produces both the will to believe and the act of believing also."[11] *The 1647 Westminster Confession* says, "All those whom God hath predestinated unto life, and those only, he is pleased, in his appointed and accepted time, effectually to call, by his Word and Spirit, out of that state of sin and death, in which they are by nature, to grace and salvation by Jesus Christ; enlightening their minds, spiritually and savingly, to understand the things of God; taking away their heart of stone, and giving unto them an heart of flesh; renewing their wills, and by his almighty power determining them to that which is good, and effectually drawing them to Jesus Christ; yet so as they come most freely, being made willing by his grace."[12] Are you regularly under the preached word? As the old-time preachers used to say, "Get under the spout where the glory comes out;" that is, under the preached word.

---

[10] "And you hath he quickened, who were dead in trespasses and sins," (Eph. 2:1).
[11] *Synod of Dort Third and Fourth Heads of Doctrine*, article 14.
[12] *The 1647 Westminster Confession of Faith*, 10:1.

John 3:16

In your regeneration there must be the general implanting of Christ. There is no regeneration without establishing the mystical union between you as a sinner and Jesus Christ as the Savior. You must be called by Jesus Christ, regenerated, joined to him as part of his elect church body, and then you will be able to hear his voice clearly.[13] Your calling by the word of God is both external and internal. In the operation of this grace by the Holy Spirit, you as the sinner are passive. The Spirit changes you (gives birth to your spirit) while the external call is going forth from the lips of the preacher who is preaching God's word. After this is accomplished, you will no longer be passive, and you will exercise faith in the message, and you will repent (a reflexive act). This repentance is also a work of grace, but it is motioned by the Spirit and accomplished by you in the midst of the change.[14] God does not believe for you, and God does not repent for you. You are motioned and moved by the Lord, and then you repent of your sin and you believe in the work of the Savior on your behalf. You are summoned by the word (which is the external call) and then you are changed in the process of the Spirit's regeneration by the application of the word to your heart (this is the internal call or what we label the

---

[13] "My sheep hear my voice, and I know them, and they follow me," (John 10:27).

[14] "Except ye repent, ye shall all likewise perish," (Luke 13:3).

effectual call). The work of the Holy Spirit on you is twofold: 1) He comes in the power of the word of God through the mouth of the faithful preacher,[15] and 2) He changes your heart by the word through illuminating your mind to the truths found in the Bible.[16]

Having heard the truth of John 2:23-3:21 the question is, do you believe what Jesus is saying and what God is teaching you in Scripture about the need to be born again? Roman Catholics, for example, hate the term "born again" because it is something they cannot participate in. Their entire system of salvation is predicated on them doing something to earn salvation. But Christ says that it is the work of the Holy Spirit that must first take place, and then you must simply believe. But believing is predicated on regeneration. And if you are regenerated, then you are already one of those for whom Christ died, the Son of Man being lifted up for *your* personal salvation. Your belief on his Gospel message is a "sure thing" once the Spirit regenerates your heart. You will have no other choice but to believe, because you now *want to believe*. A new heart has new dispositions. The Spirit's work on your heart gives you the irresistible desire to follow Christ, and to believe.

---

[15] "The *LORD'S voice* crieth unto the city," (Micah 6:9).
[16] "The eyes of your understanding being enlightened; that ye may know what is the hope of his calling, and what the riches of the glory of his inheritance in the saints," (Eph. 1:18).

John 3:16

If you are a person who thinks you are saved because you walked the isle at church, or because you were baptized as an infant into the church, or because you attend church every time the doors are open, or because your parents brought you up morally, or because you try to be a good person, or you had some "religious ecstatic experience," or for a million other reasons, then you need to take a hard look at the Pharisee of John 3. Remember, that *doing religious acts outwardly* is not the same as *having a changed heart*. Nicodemus was taken back at Christ's teaching, and he spent his whole life studying the Law of God, reading the Scriptures, attending church, doing good, trying to live a good life, *etc.* Jesus told him he was wicked, evil, and lost because his heart was not changed, just like the rest of humanity. He rebuked Nicodemus for not knowing the basics of what it meant to be regenerated – something God had been teaching the church for thousands of years.

When you die in an hour, or in a day, or in a week, or whatever time God has so set the end of your earthly life, and you stand before the Son of Man who rides on the *shekinah glory* of God, and you stand before his tribunal, and he opens the book of life and the book of conscience before you to hold you to account for all your actions, all your idle words, all your misused time, and such, and he asks you, "Why should I let you into my heaven?" what will you say to him?

Will you rest on your church attendance? Will you rest on how many times you read your bible? Will you rest on how many times you helped the old lady cross the street? Will you rest on how many bible verses you memorized in Sunday School class? Will you rest on the religious devotion you have to pray every morning, or every evening? Will you rest on trying to follow God's commandments for your life? Will you tell him that you don't lie, or don't steal or haven't murdered anyone? Will you tell him you haven't committed adultery, or haven't ever taken his name in vain or used it the wrong way? What will you tell him? What will you rest on? None of this will do you any good. As a matter for fact, if you rest in any of these things apart from the atoning work of Christ for you, on your behalf, all these things will further aggravate your sentence in the fire of eternal hell because you had a certain amount of light about God, but misused it. Such a state is worse than the unbeliever who never heard anything. Your current state is very dire indeed. Christ says you are condemned already. Judgment is already on you. And your entire life is heaping up wrath for the Day of Judgment. If you don't rest solely in what Christ accomplishes for sinners, given to sinners by the Father for atonement, what he does for them, which includes the power to be born from above, then you will spend eternity in God's hell. Hell is a place of utter darkness, where there is weeping and gnashing of teeth. It is a place where God's wrath resides forever on the souls of the impenitent – those who do not acknowledge their sinfulness and wickedness before God, and embrace Jesus Christ as Lord as given to them in the Gospel. Hell is infinitely more horrible than any painting or imagination can surmise. The presence of God in that place is his execution of just judgment on sin and wickedness – God's presence is what makes hell so horrible if you go there.[17] Most people do not realize they have a relationship with a holy God, and that relationship set within the framework of original sin in Adam, and continual sin in their acts, will be to their utter demise and eternal misery. The Bible is emphatic that there is eternal torment for sin committed against an infinite God, for an infinite duration on the never dying souls of those who go to hell. You *don't* want to go there. God says, "For a fire is kindled in mine anger, and

---

[17] Hell is "the spiritual and material furnace of fire where its damned victims, in their minds, bodies, and souls, are eternally tormented to the full degree and capacity of their beings by God, the devil and his demons, damned human beings, and themselves, through their memories and consciences, without any possibility of relief by mercy nor pity from God." Although this is a long definition of hell, it is very clear and helpful to the point at hand. It embodies all the major facets of the doctrine of eternal punishment, taught by Jesus Christ, and the reality of a literal hell." See my work, *Eternity Weighed in the Balance: The Bible's Teaching on Heaven, Hell and Salvation*, for a full discussion of this topic.

shall burn unto the lowest hell," (Deuteronomy 32:22). The Psalmist said, "The wicked shall be turned into hell and all the nations that forget God," (Psalm 9:17). Isaiah says, "Yet, thou shalt be brought down to hell…" (Isaiah 14:15). Jesus said, "How can ye escape the damnation of hell?" (Matthew 23:33). John the Apostle wrote, "And whosoever was not found written in the book of life was cast into the lake of fire," (Revelation 20:15). How can you be saved? How can you be born again? You need to acquire *a real interest* in Jesus Christ. You must depend on Christ alone for salvation which is by grace alone, through faith alone, to the glory of God alone. <u>Everything that could be good in or for us is through Jesus Christ.</u> All the benefits of salvation that God has for us are found in Christ alone. We must have an absolute dependence on Jesus Christ alone in our redemption. This is the enlightened mind resting on the work of the Holy Spirit in their heart through the Message of the Gospel of Christ's grace. It is exclusively accomplished from God's Holy Spirit that we receive the ability to exercise faith in order to have a true interest in him, "For by grace ye are saved, through faith; and that not of yourselves, it is the gift of God," (Eph. 2:8). We are totally reliant on God's power through every step of our redemption in Christ. We rely on the power of God to convert us, and give us faith in Jesus Christ, and the new nature by the power of the Holy Spirit. It is all of him.

So now what? Pray a prayer? Write your name on a card and put it in your wallet that says you "believed in his name, work and redemption for your soul?" That's what most churches would tell you to do. That way when you doubt your salvation for merely praying a prayer, you can pull that card out and remind yourself *when you prayed.* Won't that give you "lots of assurance?" No, it won't at all. Nicodemus' outward works did nothing for him that was spiritually helpful in being born again. So, what will you do now? Like Nicodemus, you are looking for true spiritual peace. Spiritual peace is a mutual concord between you and God, you who must be justified in God's sight by faith; so that your heart and God's heart are knit together in love. This results in the delightful inclination of friendship. The origin of this spiritual peace is God who originates peace with you through the Holy Spirit. It is the direct result of his mercy and love. God seeks you out, and freely offers peace to you. God subdues you in his love for you, and saves you. The consequence of gaining this spiritual peace is true friendship with God. Peace of conscience is a direct result, (Rom. 14:7; Eph. 3:12), as is peace with fellow believers, the angels and with the whole of creation, (Isa. 14:11-12; Hos. 2:18). *Your specific role with regard to spiritual peace is that you should seek spiritual peace by confessing your sins before God and to believe in Christ alone for reconciliation with God.* You should humbly submit yourself to God and remember you have a responsibility in preserving this newly gained spiritual peace. This is accomplished through your daily love for God, (John 14:21), frequent communion with God, your walk in obedience to God, (John 14:23), and return to God when you fall into sin (Jer. 3:22). Here you submit to God's providence in your life in every way. So, it's not as simple as praying a prayer and being done with it. The work of the Spirit enables you to daily cry, "Abba, Father" (Matthew 6:9; Rom. 8:15-16), which is a description of endearment to him but with great reverence, and solemnness. Together with your spirit, God will bear witness that you *are* a child of God, (Rom. 8:15-16). You will show forth the marks of a child of God. These marks are the imitation of your Father, a new life that is worthy of God and his grace, a true and sincere love for God, a devoted fear and obedience, (Mal. 1:6; 1 Pet. 1:17), and an unfeigned brotherly love. In these things you should examine yourself to be sure you possess them. Prove out your faith, exercise that faith, show forth *fruits unto righteousness*, and then never doubt your election as you *see* the fruits of that faith in your everyday life.

Finally, you must have the evidence of being born again, and you must be able to recognize its fruit. You should have, 1. A conviction of your obligation to keep the Moral Law of God found in God's Ten Commandments. "Oh how I love your law! It is my meditation all the day," (Psalm 119:97). 2. You should practice the rules of godliness and righteousness found in the Bible. "And beside this, giving all diligence, add to your faith virtue; and to virtue knowledge; and to knowledge temperance; and to temperance patience; and to patience godliness; and to godliness brotherly kindness; and to brotherly kindness charity. For if these things be in you, and abound, they make you that ye shall neither be barren nor unfruitful in the knowledge of our Lord Jesus Christ. But he that lacketh these things is blind, and cannot see afar off, and hath forgotten that he was purged from his old sins. Wherefore the rather, brethren, give diligence to make your calling and election sure: for if ye do these things, ye shall never fall," (2 Peter 1:5-10). See the progression – faith, and those attributes attached to true faith, prove out one is elected. Making your calling and election in Christ, "sure," is a product in your own heart and mind that the Spirit stirs up as a result of all those former acts of faith that you can see. 3. You should have obedience to the Law that runs in conjunction with faith in Christ. "Now the end of the commandment is charity out of a pure heart, and of a good conscience, and of faith unfeigned," (1 Tim. 1:5). 4. You must keep communion with God diligently knowing Christ is the Fountain of all grace and good works. "I am the vine, ye are the branches: He that abideth in me, and I in him, the same bringeth forth much fruit: for without me ye can do nothing," (John 15:5). You should waste no time, and do not delay. Commit yourself to Christ now, and commit your life to him for all-time.

Now, in opposition to such a notion, our Lord addresses this Jew; and it is as if he had said …

> You rabbis *say*, that when the Messiah comes, *only* the Israelites, the peculiar favorites of God, shall share in the blessings that come by, and with him. You say that the Gentiles shall reap no advantage by him, being hated of God, and rejected of him. You are mistaken. You are mistaken because you don't have a new heart. You have a hard heart, and must be born by the Spirit to even understand my words, to understand anything about my Kingdom. I tell you, God has so loved the Gentiles, as well as the Jews, that he gave his only begotten Son, to, and for them, as well as for the Jews. He is a *sure covenant* of the people, for the Gentiles as well as the Jews, and he is the Savior of them, and a sacrifice for them, a gift which is a sufficient evidence of his love to them; it being a large and

comprehensive one, an irreversible and unspeakable one. And such a Savior for Jews and Gentiles is no other than the Father's only Begotten Son, his own Son by nature, of the same essence, perfections, and glory with him. He was begotten by him in a way inconceivable and expressible by mortals. He is the true object of his love and delight, and in whom he is ever well pleased. He is the one the Father sent, not for a temporary lifting up to heal the biting of serpents on the souls of men, but one for an everlasting covenant, the sure mercies poured out over the whole world, for all kinds of men everywhere, for their salvation. And yet, such is his love towards the Gentiles, as well as the love he has for the Jews, Nicodemus, and he loved his people so much that he has given him, God in a human nature, as a sacrifice, to be lifted up, to be handed over into the hands of wicked men, to be crucified and slain as a sacrifice, as the one *given*, and to satisfy God's justice, being given to death itself for the sins of his people whom he most assuredly saves. And the good news in all this, is that whoever believes this good news, whoever believes in him, whether Jew or Gentile, shall not perish, but have everlasting life.

Other Helpful Books Published by Puritan Publications

Consider Dr. McMahon's *5 Marks* series:

5 Marks of Devotion to God
5 Marks of Biblical Reformation
5 Marks of Biblical Commitment to the Visible Body of Christ
5 Marks of a Biblical Disciple
5 Marks of a Biblical Church
5 Marks of Christian Resolve

Newly published works:

A Call to Delaying Sinners
by Thomas Doolittle (1632–1707)

A Treatise of the Loves of Christ to His Spouse
by Samuel Bolton, D.D. (1606-1654)

Attending the Lord's Table
by Henry Tozer (1602-1650)

Faith, Election and the Believer's Assurance
by George Gifford (1547-1620)

John 3:16

God is Our Refuge and Our Strength
by George Gipps (n.d.)

Remembering Your Creator
by Matthew Mead (1630-1699)

Resisting the Devil with a Steadfast Faith
by George Gifford (1547-1620)

Taking Hold of Eternal Life in Christ
by George Gifford (1547-1620)

The Believer's Marriage with Christ
by Michael Harrison (1640-1729)

The Doctrine of Man's Future Eternity
by John Jackson (1600-1648)

The Victorious Christian Soldier in Christ's Army
by Urian Oakes (1631–1681)

Zeal for God's House Quickened
by Oliver Bowles B.D. (1574-1664?)